Woman versus Won

excellent reasons for divorce but the other
the other man, need not be one of ther
message in this frank and fascinating anal
two woman battling for one man.

'An irresistible study of the way wives really feel and how they fight their replacement rivals' *Company*

'Enlightening' *Over 21*

'An analytical look at the eternal triangle from three sides . . . advocates that with the right strategy a woman can defeat her husband's mistress and win him back. Has a genuine interest and sympathy with all "victims" in her study.' *Yorkshire Post*

'*Woman versus Woman* makes controversial and essential reading for every woman and the man in her life . . . reveals the battle plan and the strategies that will defeat the mistress and win the husband back.' *Daily Mail*

'Excellent, highly readable straight reporting – often funny, often appalling – on a subject which probably impinges on most men and women during their adult lives.' *Natal Witness*

' . . . this woman war, which has been waged in secret – away from the prying eyes and tender sensibilities of men – is becoming both more common and more fierce . . . No wonder this book makes men mad.' *Toronoto Sun*

'Welcome to Shirley Eskapa's book which at last, and long overdue, confounds loaded and archaic assumptions . . . She finds that the health of the marriage has little relevance to husbands' fidelity and she coins a new phrase, "crisis of ecstasy", to describe the state of errant men who commonly leave their partners.' *Company*

' . . . plea for greater sympathy for the male libido, but also has sensible things to say about the foolishness of allowing infidelity to martial collapse.' *New Society*

'Are woman each others' natural enemies? . . . This sort of thing is not often said in the age of sisterhood so I am comforted to find a woman who is equally obsessed by what it all means . . . The case histories reveal the most bizarre campaigns, outrageous gambles, using every weapon to hand, particularly the children . . . ' *Evening Standard*

'Miss Eskapa's encounters with both the deceived and the deceiver are interesting and frightening – humans sure fight dirty when provoked.' *Sunday Times*

Novels by Shirley Eskapa

CALL BACK YESTERDAY

BLOOD FUGUE

THE SECRET KEEPER

THE SEDUCTION

SCALES OF PASSION

BLOOD RELATIONS

Woman versus Woman

SHIRLEY ESKAPA

For Inga —

Thanks for a very special evening —

Much love —

Shirley

BELLEW • LONDON

First published in Great Britain in 1984 by
William Heinemann Ltd
This revised paperback edition published in 1998 by
Bellew Publishing Company,
8 Balham Hill, London SW12 9EA

ISBN 1 85725 109 1

Printed and bound in Great Britain by
MPG Printers Ltd, Bodmin, Cornwall

For Pepo, for his wisdom

and love . . .

and to the memory of Masha

Contents

Foreword

'If only I had read your book sooner I might have saved my marriage.'

'Thank goodness I read your book in time. It gave me the confidence and the courage to save my marriage.'

One reason for responses like this when *Woman versus Woman* was first published in 1984 may be that although numerous studies, investigations and books on infidelity had been published, little if any interest had been shown in the roles played and fought out by the two women in the triangle, even though the Woman versus Woman* conflict was not a new phenomenon.

Since then much has changed. And such is the continued and growing interest in the Woman versus Woman conflict that a new edition of my long out-of-print book – with a new introduction cataloguing the changes – seems timely.

And what changes they are! For example, the slowing of the biological clock of female reproduction, *in vitro* fertilisation, surrogate mothers (rent-a-womb), Hormone Replacement Therapy (HRT), definitive paternity proof through DNA testing, the proliferation of AIDS have all added fuel to the Woman versus Woman conflict.

* For the sake of simplicity the women in a long-standing live-in relationship are referred to as wives.

Moreover, advances in the fields of information technology and communications mean that an array of new weapons has been added to the Woman versus Woman conflict. The proliferation of mobile telephones, photocopiers, fax machines and laptop computers with modems and e-mail capabilities has been put to imaginative and effective use. The last number dialled and caller display facilities of modern telephones have proved nasty traps for any number of philandering husbands and lovers with suspicious partners!

Consequently, it has been necessary to include examples of how the arsenal of new – and sometimes bizarre – tactics has been deployed. Who, ten years ago, would have dared imagine that the sperm bank and surrogate motherhood would prove to be effective attack weapons in the Woman versus Woman battle?

Today, acceptance of the deliberately conceived love child appears to go hand in hand with acceptance of the Other Woman. Just a decade ago it would have seemed as unthinkable for a man to go to court to challenge his wife's understandable wish to have an abortion as it is for twins to be conceived in a laboratory via IVF and gestated in the womb of a woman in Canada for a couple living in South Africa.

A decade or so ago it never would have occurred to the Other Woman to engage the services of a kiss-and-tell publicist such as Max Clifford to promote and profit from revealing details of her affair with a married man. Not that long ago the fabled American president John F Kennedy carried on affairs within the White House itself – and was protected from public exposure by the discretion of a respectful and deferential Press.

How different it is today for President Bill Clinton whose alleged lovers threaten to haul him before the courts! The wives of both presidents became experts at presenting a stoical front.

In those days, it is safe to assume, not even the most

resourceful Other Woman would have dreamed of employing an expert to advise her on the most effective tactic to use to net a married man and then to defeat his wife in order to take possession of him.

Publication of *Woman versus Woman* was not always welcomed. Feminists took great exception to the notion of such a conflict: the Sisterhood had put an end to that, they argued. Competitiveness and rivalry over a man were things of the past. The revolution achieved by consciousness-raising meant that the New Woman was an independent being, no longer reliant on men either materially or emotionally. It was both unprincipled and demeaning for women to fight over a man: to engage in the strategies of psychological and guerrilla warfare was positively degrading.

It was destructive to believe that the biochemistry that differentiated men from women caused significant differences in behaviour. That kind of thinking only served to perpetuate the double standard. Fortunately, marriage and the nuclear family were gradually becoming obsolete. In any case, a cheating, lying husband or partner was as undesirable as a case of herpes.

While there can be no justification for the view that the male sexual need is greater than that of the female, it is nevertheless self-defeating to try to pretend, as some feminists do, that male and female arousal mechanisms are the same.

After all, would a man who found a strange nude woman in his bedroom run for his life? Would a woman in the same situation run for hers? Or as Jessica, a cynical, high-powered investment banker in her early thirties, put it 'When a man opens his fly, his brain falls out.'

It has long been accepted that women are more in touch than men with their emotions: recent studies have attributed this to functional differences in their brains. It has also been shown that women listen with both ears, while men favour the right one And in the Woman versus Woman conflict emotion is a powerful factor.

Physically more powerful, men have always been the dominant sex despite the fact that they are more fragile and have a shorter life span. But it is not only their sexual organs and systems that differentiate between male and female bodies – for example, along with other vital differences, men cannot manufacture blood as efficiently as women. And, paradoxical as it may seem, men are three times more likely to commit suicide over a broken love affair than women.

A few journalists wrote whole pages to trash the book. Sometimes it turned out that these same journalists were Other Women.

On the other hand, as Peter van Sommers in his book *Jealousy* (Penguin 1988), referring to the incident (quoting from page 60 of *Woman versus Woman*), observed it reflects not on madness but the beginnings of a sort of ruthless sanity. He wrote:

> I read Eskapa's anecdote about the four children, the dog, the hamper and the note arriving by taxi at the husband's love-nest with great amusement but not with the falling about and crows of triumphant delight with which some of my female colleagues greeted it. (I am sure, of course, they were right.)

When more information about the horror and extent of AIDS became known, a distinguished professor of medicine, referring to the bleak prospects for finding a cure, joked bitterly: 'AIDS will make your book redundant.' But this is far from true. The consensus among researchers is that while AIDS appears to be making little impact on infidelity, it may be affecting the choice and style of affairs.

Recruiting the Other Woman, I was informed, was hardly a new phenomenon; it went back to Biblical times. Had I forgotten about Sarah, Abraham's barren wife who recruited Hagar, her maidservant and a former Egyptian princess, to bear him a child? But after the child Ishmael was born, the presence of the Other Woman disturbed Sarah and she had Hagar banished.

The concept is the same – only the shape changes.

Surrogate motherhood and recruitment of the Other Woman have taken radically new directions. See later for details of the way in which a woman similar in age to Sarah (who was said to be in her eighties) went about dealing with the same problem of an active but barren womb!

It is now little more than a decade ago since the first case of sexual harassment – an American concept but an age-old phenomenon – was brought before a tribunal.

Some dozen years ago when working for a City stockbroker, Melissa Stokes was forced to deal with sexual harassment though it hadn't yet been given a name. She discussed the problem with her boss: around four-thirty every afternoon a drunken colleague would come up behind her and grab her breasts. 'What should I do?' she asked. Firmly on her side, her boss retorted: 'Grab his balls!'

Needless-to-say, she did not take his advice – the man in question was too strong, solid and dangerous when drunk – but managed to work with him by using the time-honoured feminine ploy: false laughter.

The acceptance of sexual harassment as a punishable offence is of major importance to all women, but sadly, it has been subject to abuse.

On the whole, though, *Woman versus Woman* was enthusiastically received. It was serialised in national newspapers and magazines both in America and here. It was published in eight languages. It even appeared in the launch edition of a national American women's magazine. It grew in popularity: four years after it was published, Oprah Winfrey sent for me twice to appear on her show.

As a result, women from all over the world contacted me. The youngest Other Woman to get in touch was sixteen, the oldest seventy-four, while the oldest wife in the Woman versus Woman conflict was eighty-three.

Most rewarding of all, however, was the knowledge that doctors, psychologists marriage counsellors and even divorce lawyers recommended the book to their patients or clients to help them deal with the Woman versus Woman conflict.

Here, for example, is what Dr Arnold A Lazarus, Distinguished Professor of Psychology at America's Rutgers University, had to say:

> In the arena of marital discord, the words *Woman versus Woman* tend to conjure up the image of the downtrodden wife who has served and nurtured her faithless husband, only to be rewarded by rejection and abandonment in the wake of a much younger replacement.
>
> When faced with evidence of infidelity, most wives tend to become confrontational, others ignore or deny the situation; some silently brood over it, and many try to devise a plan to save the marriage.
>
> In this engaging and enlightening book, Shirley Eskapa lucidly and poignantly takes us into and beyond these familiar scenarios. With evidence derived from case studies and careful interviews she amplifies the politics of jealousy by furnishing a number of amazing manoeuvres some women resort to when fighting back.

The march of science has made a significant impact on the Woman versus Woman conflict. When interviewed at the age of fifty-three about her third affair with a married man, Baroness (Margaret) Jay, daughter of former Labour Prime Minister Lord Callaghan, told Rebecca Hardy of the *Daily Mail* that HRT means we no longer have to accept the stereotypes of the ageing, superfluous middle-aged woman. No longer entirely accurate is Aristophanes' observation that a man, though grey-haired, can always get himself a wife, but a woman's time is short.

Its seems that HRT cannot only prolong the sensuality of

some women but also extend the period of female reproduction, resulting in the pregnancy of at least two women in their early sixties. Less bizarrely, the biological clock has slowed and women who fall pregnant at the age of forty-six are scarcely a rarity.

Both wives and the Other Woman were intrigued and on occasion refreshed, encouraged, warmed, delighted, amused and shocked by the account of the creative tactics of vengeance they read about in *Woman versus Woman*. Many, in fact, wrote in telling me of their most satisfying ways of getting even.

Mayline, thirty-eight, an account executive for an engineering group: 'I knew that Pam, my treacherous best friend, had suffered several allergic reactions to flea powder. It was easy enough for me to gain entry to her flat, so I went in and sprinkled flea powder over her knickers.

'I didn't get my husband back – to this day I'm not sure I even wanted to – but it made me feel less of a powerless victim, less damaged. It was a kind of retaliation and it made me feel better about myself.'

Val, forty-three, an interior designer, used this ploy to force her rival, Geraldine, into an angry confrontation with her husband.

> She spent three days tailing me in my Ford escort while driving the convertible BMW my husband had lent her while he was abroad. I tricked her into following me into two of our friends' houses. I thought it would be a good thing if they saw her taunting me. I knew they would be sufficiently outraged to tell Edward what they had seen. That was five years ago.
>
> Since then neither Edward nor I have mentioned the incident. I think he secretly admired me for my daring.

Less amusing was the Other Woman who spread the rumour at work that her rival had AIDS. But the wife who informed the authorities that her husband's Polish mistress was in the country illegally succeeded in having her deported.

Carol, a wife with a major weight problem, was deluged by advertisements for slimming foods and videos sent by Kim, her husband's mistress (Carol was never able to prove this).

When her husband's affair had ended, Gail, a recovering alcoholic in her late thirties, received three bottles of her favourite expensive whisky *after* her husband returned home. This led to a near tragic setback. See page 153 for other examples of the behaviour of jilted Other Women.

Part of the fascinating horror of the spine-chilling movie *Fatal Attraction,* leading up to the attempt of the Other Woman to kill the wife in her bath, was the scene where the wife discovers the rabbit boiled to death in her own kitchen. Again, the act of vengeance took place *after* the affair had ended.

With her ten-year affair finally over, Maria, the Other Woman, hand-delivered to Jean the letters describing intimate erotic details that Dick had written to her during their time together.

Whenever Nina, founder of a well-known head hunting company, went abroad on business, she left a note in her bathroom: 'Whoever you are, please replace the lids on my creams after you have used them.' She wanted the Other Woman 'to know that I knew, and that she was just one of several'.

Terry and Ben had a tiny seaside cottage in Cornwall. When she first suspected he was using it as a venue for trysts with his secretary, she, too, left a note in the drinks cupboard: 'One of these bottles is poisoned'.

Yet another wife faxed a brief message to the Other Woman at the hotel where she knew she and her husband were spending a weekend: 'Please make sure he goes to the loo. He suffers from terrible constipation. This happens to men when they're over sixty. If he does not go he will make your life a misery. A lovely young thing like you deserves better.'

When Sue, the Other Woman, ended the affair with her married lover Ted because she was bored with his constant preoccupation with his wife's depression over the death of her mother, she left this message on their answer phone: 'Get yourself a real therapist and a new bathrobe. Stop wearing your mother's tired old baby-pink dressing gown. Ted can't take it any more.'

As soon as she identified her, Lucy contacted the Other Woman and rapidly told her that she had already informed Janette and Mary and Charlotte and others that she was ready to divorce her husband just as soon as he wished. 'If he's not leaving me for you, it isn't because I'm standing in his way, but because he doesn't want to. I'm an excuse, not a reason.'

The anecdote on page 61 about a wife who sent their four children and a dog in a taxi to the love-nest where her husband and very young lover were living attracted extraordinary attention. Those who responded negatively felt that such sly and deceitful conduct was an insult to women, but in the main the comment was enthusiastic.

I include here a similar successful ploy.

Shelly, a freelance editor, thirty-nine, was married for sixteen years to Dennis, forty-five, an engineer. They had two daughters, eight and ten.

> Dennis left us the day after Christmas. Almost three months later, my straightlaced mother who believes that honesty is the best policy and a white lie is still a lie, sent me a copy of *Woman versus Woman*. She taped a note on the cover instructing me to turn to page 61. As I read it, for the first time since he had gone, I laughed out loud.
>
> The next day she called to ask whether I'd got the book and had I read page 61. It's not exactly cheap to laugh long distance but that is what we did. She told me she had a campaign plan. She wanted me to spend Easter with her and my father in Glasgow and leave the girls to stay with Dennis and that bimbo-executive – as I called Juliette.

I was a bit reluctant as I'd never been able to bring myself to go away without my daughters. My mother didn't even try to conceal her irritation. She was rather tart – perhaps once, just once I should put my husband first? I was taken aback – she'd never interfered before, so I listened to her very carefully.

She had decided that I should get a bad dose of 'flu, but while we were talking, she changed her mind. 'Flu wouldn't do at all – it would have to be pneumonia. On Easter Sunday she would tell Dennis I'd come down with pneumonia.

I sat beside her while she phoned and curtly informed him that I was too ill to travel. Pneumonia is what happens to people who are run down, she told him. Stress, too much stress, of course, makes everything worse, and from what she heard there was no shortage of stress in her daughter's life. He called every day to find out how I was getting on. By Saturday we got the call we were waiting for: he told us the girls had moved back to our house – Juliette's flat was too small . . .

I stayed on in Glasgow for another five days. Mother and I had quite a bit of fun, too. We became very close. One afternoon while my father was working in their beloved garden she told me he had once fallen head over heels for a woman – a bus driver called Mavis. It was hard to believe. My stern and kindly father who used to be a bank manager had an affair? Silence was the best weapon, she said, and she had used it well. That, and patience. And my father never knew that she'd made up her mind, in her heart of hearts, that she would wait one year and not a minute longer.

Dennis and the girls were waiting at Heathrow. It turned out that while Sophie and Holly had been fighting, they'd knocked over one of Juliette's porcelain ornaments. When Holly spilt Juliette's nail polish over her white carpet, it was the straw that broke the camel's back. Juliette had a terrible temper.

> I let Dennis stay in the house, but didn't take him back immediately. That might have given the game away and I couldn't risk it.

In 1983, shortly before the publication of *Woman versus Woman*, Sara Keays, middle aged and pregnant, following revelations in the Press about her affair with Cecil Parkinson, the then Secretary of State for Trade & Industry and chairman of the Conservative Party, felt compelled to tell her side of the story. *The Times* had chided Parkinson for having made a sad and silly blunder: only three days later the *Telegraph* stated that a quiet abortion is greatly to be preferred to a scandal.

Justifiably incensed and well-schooled in the ways of the political world, Sara Keays rightly timed her retaliation during the week of the Conservative Party conference when the potential for danger to Parkinson was greatest. He announced his resignation from the party post while the conference was still in progress.

Parkinson's public tribute to his wife, Ann, was greeted by huge headlines Even so, he was largely condemned not for cheating on his wife but for cheating on his mistress. But a disgruntled cast-off mistress, even one with a tragically handicapped child, can't keep an ambitious man down. Recently Parkinson, who was made a life peer in 1992, emerged from the political wilderness to become chairman of the Conservative Party – yet again. He is known as a strategist!

Although no one can ever know what Ann Parkinson's quietly dignified and even noble defence of her family cost her, scores of wives, similarly invaded, took great comfort and strength from her example of fortitude and loyalty.

It seems the wife rarely, if ever, uses the media as an instrument for revenge. When Jilly Cooper, the best-selling and good-natured novelist, confided in a journalist friend that there had been a marital hiccup when her husband Leo had a dalliance, the Other Woman, Sarah Johnson, a publisher's assistant, interpreted this as a snide, planned attack even though her name had not been mentioned.

She retaliated by deploying the *Guardian* to expose the intimate details of her eight-year-long affair with Leo, saying, 'As she (Jilly) seems intent on prolonging my pain I feel that I can no longer remain silent.' Her story was even sold to the *Daily Mirror* – yet another case of the continuation of the Woman versus Woman conflict *after* the relationship has ended. Such an attack is both effective and profitable.

When Mary Ellen Synon's three-year affair with Rupert Pennant-Rea, deputy governor of the Bank of England, ended and she went public, his resignation was as certain as she could have wished it to be.

Had he kept his promises to her – promises he was in no position to make – she might not have exposed the lurid details of their affair, such as making love on the floor of the Governor's dressing room at the Bank. She also made public Pennant-Rea's letters describing the kind of sexual fantasies most people would never admit to.

But it took a year of letters to various journalists and publications before Mary Ellen, a journalist herself, succeeded in bringing him down.

Pennant-Rea's wife Helen was nothing if not stoic. In a prepared statement she said: 'His relationship with Miss Synon ended over a year ago and Rupert told me about it then. Over the last year, despite her threat to publicise the affair, we have endeavoured to rebuild our marriage and protect all our children. Rupert has paid a very high price for making the right decision and staying with us.'

It would seem, therefore, that had Pennant-Rea complied with Mary Ellen's threats or blackmail – he could have had both his career *and* her. In which case the price would have been even more exorbitant: it might have bankrupted his soul.

As a pre-emptive measure, Nanette, married to an unusually handsome and dynamic banker who travels the world, goes in for black humour. 'Just remember, Mrs Bobbit got off,' she warns him. 'If your lady goes public like Pennant-Rea's girl friend I might even take the Bobbit route.' As far as she knows there have been no girlfriends. 'But you never can tell – I hope I've frightened the life out of him!' What man wouldn't tread a straight and narrow path under the ultimate threat by his wife to cut off his penis?

Several wives have made liberal use of the powers of publicity, warning their husbands that the media have the power to end their careers.

Sara Keays, Mary Ellen Synon and Sarah Johnson did not need the kiss-and-tell services of the publicist, Max Clifford, who can charge clients between £4,000 and £7,000 a month to either get their names into the tabloids or, alternatively, to keep them out. In 1993 the actress Antonia de Sancha availed herself of his expertise to expose the intimate details of her affair with then Tory MP David Mellor, Minister for Sport, who according to somewhat ribald Press accounts, made love to her wearing his Chelsea Football Club regalia. Ironically, though Clifford, a Christian who deplores hypocrisy, turned her into a fleeting celebrity, it was Mellor who became a prominent media personality.

One of Clifford's more tragic interventions was when he helped Marian Smith, a married woman and a mother of three, publicise her affair with her GP, Keith Pilsworth, also married and the father of three, *after the affair was over.*

No official complaint was lodged with the General Medical Council until the affair ended. Because Dr Pilsworth had contravened medical ethics by sleeping with his patient, he was struck off the medical register. (Almost a year later, following an enthusiastic and dedicated campaign by his patients, he was reinstated).

Even worse befell his family as the tale unfolded. Imagine the pain as Marian Smith's revelations, along with a photograph of her wearing a tee-shirt emblazoned with the vulgar slogan 'I've been doctored', appeared in a down-market

Sunday tabloid. Although Marian Smith had consensual sex with her doctor, she was still seen as a victim. The doctor had, after all, taken advantage of the intimacy essential to the doctor-patient relationship. Interestingly, Marian Smith coloured and styled her hair so she looked remarkably like Jennie, the doctor's wife. (It is not unknown in the Woman versus Woman conflict for a wife to take the same step and redesign herself in the style of the Other Woman).

In a tragic sequel, the Pilsworths' only son Tim, aged twenty-seven and also a doctor, was incurably damaged by watching his father being destroyed by the lurid publicity. He committed suicide.

Jennie Pilsworth's intelligent and sympathetic account of her husband's affair is as moving as it is inspirational. 'Adversity,' she told Frances Hardy of the *Daily Mail,* 'has made us stronger. But the strain of it all has been horrendous. It has nearly wiped us out.'

Today, the belief that an affair with a married man is not only unforgivably immoral but also a personal catastrophe too shameful to speak of is barely a distant memory.

Former South African circuit judge James Harkness and his wife Valerie used Clifford to reveal how former Tory minister Alan Clark seduced Valerie along with her two grown daughters Alison (Ali) and Josephine (Joei) – the 'coven', as Clark, an incorrigible ladies' man, had christened the trio in his earlier best-selling *Diaries*.

As with the kiss-and-tell exposé of Mellor, any hurt inflicted on the malefactor's family appears to have been irrelevant. Harkness, who called for Clark to be horse-whipped, flew from Cape Town to London for the sole purpose of canvassing for New Labour against Clark who, despite the judge's efforts and with the continuing support of his long-suffering wife Jane, was elected MP for Kensington and Chelsea.

A recent *Company* magazine cover story promised readers a guaranteed method to meet and steal a married man away from his wife – for £100 a day. After a brilliantly successful campaign to destroy her present husband's previous wife and daughter, Sarah X decided to set up an agency to teach women how to dispense with a wife and annihilate a marriage. In Sarah's view 'getting a man is like going to war – you need fox-like cunning and nerves of steel.' She added: 'When a mistress comes to me, the wife of the guy concerned had better watch out . . . I often get asked if I'm concerned if the man has kids. The answer is "no".'

Superb cosmetic surgery combined with excellent health and a sparkling wit have kept mega-rich Florence Hammond slim, curvaceous and, even in her eighties, undeniably pretty.

It is generally believed that but for a certain dignity – an unmistakable delicacy she would have looked ridiculous.

When she was seventy-eight she married Thomasino Bozzoni, an insurance broker, who at forty-five was thirty-three years her junior. Much to the amazement of everyone who knew them, the marriage seemed to work. They played poor bridge and worse golf, but orchid growing was their real passion.

Five years later, when Thomasino turned fifty and Florence, eighty-three, he began to speak of his longing for a child. This sudden longing appeared to have begun when he met Gina, a rather ordinary looking waitress at their golf club.

Florence, it seemed, could supply him with everything but his own child. Undaunted, she set about neutralising Gina's fertile advantage – she researched the mechanics of renting a womb (location, costs, etc) and then offered him fatherhood with the same generosity she had offered him a Ferrari. Thomasino graciously accepted.

The womb belonged to a woman in a distant state who already had three children The artificial insemination was successful and approximately eight months later Florence and Thomasino returned to Ohio to be present at the birth of his child, a son they named Mario after his grandfather.

Proof of Thomasino's gratitude was the expulsion of Gina.

Now three years old and the apple of his parents' eyes, Mario lives a life of uncontrolled luxury. Gina's weapon of fertility was neutralised. She conceded victory to Florence. Magnanimous as always, Florence sweetened her defeat. (Paying off the other woman is a tactic as old as the Woman versus Woman conflict).

Equally unusual is the war between Norah Parker, the seventy-four-year-old Other Woman, and Maureen Marshall, the wife aged sixty-seven, over the affection and attention of her husband Gerald, aged seventy-one. Though at the lower end of the socioeconomic spectrum, Norah, too, used finance as a weapon. She began by giving Gerald her dead husband's socks, shirts, jackets and silver pencils.

Then, when the Parkers' car was in need of costly repairs and it was doubtful it would pass the MOT test, Norah, who could not drive, bought a car. It was then that Gerald moved in to live with her, leaving Maureen to continue to look after his seventy-eight-year-old invalid brother who lived with them.

Although they all lived in a small town, the only chance meeting between the two women took place in a wool shop. When Maureen saw Norah, she said loudly, 'Look what the cat's dropped in!' Norah went white and asked for wool. 'It's a pity you didn't stick to your knitting in the first place,' Maureen remarked bitterly.

Still distressed because she made no move to retaliate physically – 'I should have scrubbed those wrinkled cheeks of hers' – Maureen sees no solution to her problem. Even were Norah to die, her presence would haunt their lives, Maureen would have to live with Gerald's grief.

Here is further example of medical technology as a weapon.

When Amy was twenty-six, after she and Hans, thirty-three, had been married for five years, the doctors told her that a malformed uterus meant she would never bear a child. A highly successful restaurateur who already owned a string of restaurants, Hans adored his unusually beautiful and intelligent wife and wanted to have a child with her and no one else. Adoption was out of the question.

Blonde, blue-eyed and stereotypically Aryan, they were so well matched they even looked alike. Hans' mother was German, his father Welsh. Amy's parents had been true-blue Brits for generations.

Some two years after their devastating news, Amy hit on a radical idea. Hans was then thirty-five and, therefore, as she reassured him, his sperm was still highly fertile. (Recent reports in the media about low sperm counts had made her aware of the possibility of male infertility). She begged him to deposit his sperm in a sperm bank where it could be frozen in case some medical miracle made it possible for her to conceive and bear a child. When he disagreed, she appeared to have a nervous breakdown. Finally, he capitulated and she went on to lead a satisfying and highly fulfilled life developing her newly discovered talent as a sculptor.

Amy freely admitted to herself that she had never been overwhelmed by a maternal instinct and had only wanted a child for Hans' sake. Even before they were married he had told her how much he loved and wanted children. Greedy for all his love and affection, she secretly rejoiced in her childlessness.

They had been married for twelve years when she saw Hans take a lighted cigarette and hand it to Katie – one of his attractive restaurant managers – who immediately put it between her lips. That small intimacy signalled danger, and Amy took immediate action.

She had not, until then, known exactly why she had urged him to freeze his sperm. An instant plan (formed, perhaps, unconsciously over several years?) presented itself to her. The following three months saw her intensively investigating how to put her bizarre plan into action.

The next time Hans went to New York on a three-week business trip, she did not accompany him as she usually did.

There was no problem about Katie – as a single parent she could never travel far from her five-year-old daughter who suffered from epilepsy. Instead, she collected Hans' frozen sperm and flew with it to Berlin, to the surrogate mother whose blonde, blue-eyed looks conformed to her requirements. She wanted the child to have the closest possible resemblance to Hans. She returned to London and learned three weeks later that the artificial insemination had resulted in a pregnancy.

Once a month for the next five months she flew to Berlin to make sure all was going well. Three weeks before the due-date she and the surrogate mother flew to London to await the birth. Her overwhelming concern was how and when to tell Hans. Haunted by a belated recognition of the dangerous consequences inherent in what she had done, she was in a state of unremitting terror. She now knew she had misinterpreted Hans' sharing of a cigarette and this, ironically enough, made everything worse.

In the end, of course, she had to tell him.

He thought, at first, that if she were not joking, she must be crazy, for surely she could not have deceived him like this, done anything so cruel, so murderous, so *uncivilised*? Because it couldn't be true that she could be guilty of a violation so destructive, so inhuman, that it went, unforgivably, beyond the comprehension of any normal human being? But when she told him, in answer to his question, that she had paid £35,000, it became clear she was deadly serious. It was then that Hans – whose rapid decisiveness had always been one of his greatest assets – told her all future communications would come from his lawyer. The next moment he turned on his heel and walked out.

As good as his word, she did not see or hear from him for three months. Three days after the baby was born Amy brought her to a home without Hans. She had already engaged a nanny – she still had *no* maternal feelings, but felt she would not have Hans' child adopted. She called the child Heidi after Hans' mother.

She did not consider his behaviour undeserved.

Meanwhile, Heidi's resemblance to her father grew more pronounced and by the time she was three months old, she was his mirror image. That was when Amy took Heidi with her and marched unannounced into Hans' office. She wanted him to look at the child, she would ask for nothing more.

He looked, he saw and could not stop himself from taking the baby into his arms.

Hans still does not know about the fateful cigarette. Amy still insists, privately, that she has no maternal instinct. But Hans, it seems, has more than enough for both of them.

Kelly, fifty-two, formerly a legal secretary but now a housewife and voluntary hospital worker, married to Seth, fifty-five, an investment banker, was shocked when she found herself feeling sympathy for her husband who broke into tears when he confessed to having an affair with Cindy, twenty-eight, an unmarried laboratory assistant and daughter of a distant acquaintance:

> Early one morning I awoke about five, and discovered Seth was not in bed beside me. Naturally, I was anxious. This was unusual to say the least. So of course I got up at once to look for him. I found him sitting at the kitchen table, in the dark, actually *sobbing.*
>
> I thought he might be ill or in horrible pain. I'd never seen him really cry before. When I asked him if he was ill or in pain, he couldn't answer. He just shook his head. Problems at work? Had he been gambling? Were we in debt? He continued to shake his head. And then, I'll never know why, I said, 'You're not having an affair, are you?' He nodded his head and cried even louder.
>
> Although I wanted to throw him out, I was sorry for him, so I made us some tea and brought it to him, and he calmed down a bit. Then the story came tumbling out.
>
> Briefly: it had been going on for about four months, he

didn't love her and never had, he wanted out, but she was blackmailing him, threatening him that if he broke up with her, she would tell *me*. He was sure I'd divorce him if I found out.

I didn't know exactly how or what I felt about divorcing or not divorcing, but I knew she had to stop this blackmail.

Seth did not go to the office. Within a couple of hours we decided what to do. Later that day we faxed Cindy at work – open-plan offices. The fax stated: 'My husband Seth has informed me that you will tell me all about his adultery with you if he breaks up with you. Stop blackmailing him! I know everything I need to know. Kelly Walker.'

When it was typed I gave it to Seth. He wrote by hand, the following: 'I have one more thing to say. Leave me alone. Please don't ever think about coming near me.'

The following day I sent a fax to her parents.

Kelly and Seth decided to relate this episode to their own daughters. It gives them great delight to tell everyone that they are happier than they have ever been.

The next account is one of the more satisfying consequences of having written *Woman versus Woman.*

When, after much agonising, Ralph finally left Philippa, the mother of his two children with whom he had been living for ten years, to go away with Beverly, it was at Philippa's suggestion.

Philippa had decided to follow Clare's example, (page 65), 'to take away at least one vital ingredient from her (ie, the Other Woman's) magic potion. She took away the element of the clandestine, the forbidden!'

Since Ralph and Beverly had never spent more than a night at a time together. Philippa hoped that 'a little bit of daily contact would take away the thrilling risk of my finding out as well as the urgency of having a few snatched hours together.

'In other words, although they would be living in an hotel

and there would be no housekeeping, ordinary, routine, necessary things like washing socks and underwear would still have to go on,' she observed. 'Men may send their socks to the hotel laundry but as a rule, women do not send their tights.'

Ralph's secretary, Lily, a hearty woman, was given to mothering both of them. Her only daughter lived in Canada and Philippa often invited her to their home for Sunday lunch when Ralph was out of town. The phone and the fax kept Ralph and Lily in constant touch.

After ten days of interrupted bliss, Lily included in a lengthy fax of a contract, a photocopy of the relevant page, from *Woman versus Woman*. Amused, Ralph went into the bathroom and, sure enough, Beverly's tights were hanging on a line over the bath.

The next day – this time at his request – Lily sent a tense fax informing him of an emergency meeting. Clearly, Ralph had no choice but to return to the boardroom immediately.

On the plane Ralph was quiet and thoughtful. Naturally, Beverly asked him what was wrong. Politely, but firmly, he let her know that things hadn't gone quite as he had expected; he had made a terrible mistake, and now he could only hope and pray that Philippa would take him back.

Lily never told him how she had come to send the page she had photocopied from *Woman versus Woman*. Whether he solved that mystery for himself remains anyone's guess.

Tina, an advertising agency copywriter, was twenty when the affair with her boss, Simon, broke up. She brought a case of sex harassment against him, alleging that he had initiated the affair with no encouragement from her – by groping her breasts in the filing room. It emerged that all the encouragement had come from her. When asked why she had done this, she responded with a question: 'Why should his wife go around thinking she was married to a faithful Mr Nice Guy?' But what did his wife have to do with it? The reply: 'She was the one who'd got him.'

One of the most public of Other Women is Camilla Parker Bowles, mistress of the Prince of Wales. With the tragic death at the age of thirty-six of Diana, Princess of Wales, his divorced wife and mother of his two sons, the way appears clear at last for Camilla to marry her prince and England's future king.

Diana, a fairy tale, virginal bride was nineteen when she married Charles. What she didn't know was that Charles had failed to put Camilla Parker Bowles, his long-time love, behind him. Just before the wedding Diana came upon a gold bracelet with a blue enamel disc engraved with the initials F and G – standing for 'Fred' and 'Gladys', names Charles and Camilla called each other. It was a present from Charles to his mistress. If that weren't enough, Charles wore gold cufflinks engraved with entwined 'Cs' – for Charles and Camilla on their honeymoon. They were a present from Camilla. The final affront came when Charles opened his diary and photographs of Camilla fell out.

These intrusions shocked the young Diana and made it clear that Camilla was a major part of her new husband's life. Camilla and Brigadier Andrew Parker Bowles, her now former husband, apparently enjoyed what was once called an 'open' marriage. He, at any rate, became known as 'the man who laid down his wife for his country'.

One of the Other Woman's most effective ploys is to persuade the wife to doubt her own sanity. When Diana suffered from severe postnatal depression after Prince William's birth, she was, by her own account, labelled 'unstable' and 'mentally unbalanced' by members of the Royal Family. Then came the eating disorder. Having assumed that Charles would keep his assurances to cool his friendship with Camilla, it was not at all surprising that her suspicions about Charles's and Camilla's continuing relationship appeared to her so outrageous, so unreasonable, that she began to doubt her own sanity. Camilla, in fact, was never far away; should Diana press the last number called on Charles' portable phone. Chances were she'd find herself connected to the Parker Bowles residence.

When she came upon Camilla Parker Bowles' letters to Charles written on *her* headed notepaper, she had the grim satisfaction of proving to herself that her suspicions were not those of a jealous wife who had lost her reason. By then she was wracked by *bulimia nervosa* brought on, as she herself explained, by low self-esteem when 'you don't think you're worthy or valuable.' It was a terrible situation and Diana knew it. 'Well,' she told the BBC, 'there's no better way to dismantle a personality than to isolate it.'

Superior in experience and expertise, Camilla Parker Bowles cunningly plotted and achieved the demolition of her enemy, rendering Diana's beauty, which could have made her unassailable, not only useless but counter-productive. Beside a horsy, stodgy, countrified Camilla, the elegant Diana was deemed frivolous. Had she been less beautiful, she would have been more acceptable – but to Charles' 'Highgrove Set', her beauty, like her spontaneous compassion, was considered extreme. As she herself put it, in their world, she was 'a non-starter'. The result was predictable. 'Well, there were three of us in this marriage,' she told the BBC in 1995, 'so it was a bit crowded.' But it was Diana, not Camilla, who was the outsider She was different from the usual cool, if not cold, controlled Englishwoman of her class.

She explained: 'Because I do things differently, because I don't go by the rule book, because I lead from the heart, not the head, and albeit that's got me in trouble with my work, I understand that. But someone's got to go out there and love people and show it.'

Camilla Parker Bowles won the Woman versus Woman conflict, destroying Diana as a wife and future queen. But she lost the war. The world will long remember Diana for the love she showered on the loveless and bereft. She became known as the 'people's princess' for her charitable work, a woman for whom no one was too humble or sick for a smile or even a cuddle.

Now a widower, Charles is free to marry Camilla who, as

the publicly-acknowledged mistress to a future king, came out of the shadows and acquired a social secretary to juggle her increasingly busy life. In the weeks before Diana's death Charles' and Camilla's relationship was polished by the 'Highgrove Set', one example being a long article in the prestigious *New Yorker* magazine called 'Love in a Cold Climate' which appeared to put a stamp of approval on their enduring affair. The coldness of the climate in which *they* live is, perhaps, illustrated by the fact that the Royal Family's statement on Diana's death failed to mention sorrow or grief.

If the Woman versus Woman conflict is fuelled by hatred of the Other Woman, this is because it is far easier to focus the fear, distortion and rage that make up the hatred on to her rather than the husband. It is also safer – the denial of a husband's responsibility makes it far easier to forgive and on occasion even sympathise with him.

Women fantasise more frequently over punishing, injuring or even killing their rivals rather than the men who have betrayed them. Typically, some women cannot keep this a controlled fantasy and have gone so far as to murder their rivals.

One woman confessed to a longing to put rat poison in her rival's sugar but when it occurred to her that her husband might stir the poisoned sugar into his own tea she instantly dropped the fantasy.

Despite the bitter enmity of the two warring women in the Woman versus Woman conflict, women are, in the main, the greatest allies – sharing sadness and joy, spreading solace and wisdom – fully aware that, as Francis Bacon observed, 'those who have no friends to open themselves unto are cannibals of their own hearts.'

Since publication of *Woman versus Woman,* the conventional wisdom that only those marriages that are weak and crumbling are susceptible to the Other Woman is more and more recognised to be a dangerous myth. So what does a shocked, demoralised wife do?

In the words of Rutgers' Dr Lazarus:

> Perhaps the main message of *Woman versus Woman* is to transform, whenever possible, the bland rage of hurt, indignation and anger into strategic battle lines. Unbridled attacks on the recreant partner tend to further jeopardise the relationship because they make the assailant seem even more unattractive. If possible, when trying to salvage her marriage, success is most likely to follow the wife who manages to convert stereotypic rivalry and hatred into human-to-human recognition.

Acknowledgements

I am profoundly grateful to all those men and women who gave so generously (and, frequently, so painfully) of their heartfelt experiences in the Woman versus Woman conflict.

Several people engaged in the writing and publishing professions gave me enormous encouragement. I first discussed the concept of the book with Margaret Pringle (then Doubleday's London editor) who went to great lengths to urge me to go ahead. Sometimes authors are lucky enough to have the skills of an editor available to them, and although Patrick Cosgrave was no longer my official editor, he read the typescript again and again and his criticism was invaluable. Jane Turnbull, who commissioned *Woman versus Woman* allowed me enormous latitude as well as offering constant encouragement. Janet Law contributed in no small measure to the final draft. My agent, Mark Lucas, was infinitely patient. Jillian Becker gave not only constructive comment but endless encouragement. Lee-Anne Isaacs was an indefatigable research assistant, and Joan Robson deciphered and typed several drafts. Nicholas Stacey read an early draft and this was more helpful than I can say.

Bea Tollman, whose unfailing compassion has seen me through many trying times, saw me through this one too. Suzi Kessler, a physician in the truest sense contributed her inimitable logic. Anette and Derek Nunn allowed me to make the most of their special skills. Halena Szpiro, a wise and incorrigible student of life, gave of her penetrating insight, and Rosalie Berwin gave me the benefit of her legal and gentle wisdom.

But of course the burden of living with me fell to my own family. My sister, Rhona Beck, was tireless in her concern, encouragement and perceptive comment; my children, Roy, Linda and Robert were not only forbearing but interested.

My inexpressible gratitude goes to my husband, Raymond, who, although mentioned last, is and always has been first, and who allowed his very soul to be pressed into the service of *Woman Versus Woman*.

Introduction

The Woman versus Woman conflict is the battle that ensues when two women go to war over one man. It is, of course, an immemorial conflict, as mysterious as it is ancient. It is a battle, principally, of identity, whether it is fought by the wife from within the family, or by the Other Woman from without. And, more often than not, it is a battle in which lives are damaged, hearts broken and which no one really wins. No general approaches war with anything like the profound enmity of one woman warring against another over a man. And no secret service agent would approach his or her assignment with a fraction of the fascination, ingenuity, curiosity, and passionate bitterness of one woman doing battle with another.

The conventional wisdom that it is only those marriages that are weak and crumbling which are susceptible to the Other Woman is a dangerous myth. It goes without saying that a weak marriage is more vulnerable than a strong one, and yet nothing is as confounding as when the 'Ideal Couple' falls to the Other Woman just as finally as the 'Ordinary Couple'.

It was only after I had seen what everyone who knew them – friends, relations, the wife herself, and the children – believed to be the Ideal Couple fall to the Other Woman, that I began to think seriously about this phenomenon. 'Her husband ran off with another woman' is, of course, a familiar phrase, but I began to wonder about men, about what makes them susceptible to the influence of the Other Woman, and about what attempts were made to encourage them to stay with their wives. I began to wonder about the wives, how they responded; and about the Other Women – what made them so cruelly clever? Being a wife, I started with little or no sympathy for the Other Woman, but after talking to five or six of them this changed. I have subsequently talked to at least 150 Other Women from all walks of life and I found that all those who had engaged in what I later called the Woman versus Woman conflict were ordinary people, neither especially cruel nor especially clever.

Once I started discussing the subject – and in the last four years I have interviewed over 400 people – I found that everyone has some sort of theory; I never once came across anyone who was indifferent to it.

Of course, many men leave desperately unhappy, strifetorn marriages for the Other Woman. And yet, many I spoke to said they would not have left even those bitter marriages if they had not found someone else. Other men reported that they had left a marriage that was *not* unhappy and regretted it; they now felt that if they and their wives had understood more of their dilemma, their present unhappiness might have been avoided. Notably few said that they had found 'true happiness'.

And how do their wives respond? Some are too hurt or too angry to make any coherent attempt to save their marriages; others go to war and formulate ingeniously effective strategies; while others still are delighted to rid themselves of tiresome husbands and even go to great lengths to recruit the Other Woman to make this possible.

Until quite recently, the Woman versus Woman conflict has been shrouded in secrecy and so it has never been subjected to any sort of systematic analysis. It is a conflict, after all, that threatens the basic unit of human life – the couple or family. It is therefore biological as well as societal.

The Woman versus Woman conflict has been kept secret from most men, though not all. Its design and style have always been better understood by women than by men, largely because it has been kept so secret. But the growth in the number of Other Women and the accompanying tragedy of many of them has meant that notwithstanding the secrecy of the Woman versus Woman conflict, it warrants scrutiny. It is never a pretty fight, and, since it will undoubtedly expose many of women's better kept secrets to men, it will raise considerable anger.

I am aware that in writing a book of this nature I am going against current trends. Women are not supposed to fight to keep a man, nor are they supposed to fight each other over a man. It may be that in many respects *Woman versus Woman* shows women in an all too human and far from flattering light, and many liberated women will consider the writing of this book to be an act of treachery. There will be others who will claim that *Woman versus Woman* only compounds what they see as the evils of the women's movement. But it is only because the Other Woman has become so prevalent that this book came to be written in the first place.

This undertaking is not underpinned by any special qualifications. I have a BA degree with a major in Sociology and a sub-major in Psychology; later I took a postgraduate degree in International Relations which included Strategic Studies.

Woman versus Woman reflects the personal experiences of the more than 400 people who were interviewed. The stories presented here are a fraction of the total number I was told. All the stories are true. I spoke to winners, losers and survivors. Many of them you will know from personal experience; some you will recognize; many of them you will comprehend for the first time. The analysis of background and strategies inherent in the Woman versus Woman conflict is the source of unexpected enlightenment for both women and men. And whether or not you find the tactics of the women involved pitiful or smart, meretricious, distasteful, amusing, tragic or triumphant, you will not fail to find them instructive. All the names of the people have been disguised including all those who specifically requested that they should not be disguised.

The rising intensity of the Woman versus Woman conflict is one of the most devastating consequences of the sexual revolution. The advance of the women's movement and the sexual freedom granted by contraception have caused more and more women to spend more time in an undefined and uncertain no-man's-land where they are trapped, not liberated, in a battle which rages between them and inside themselves. In the fight for basic human equality, differences in male and female sexual responses have been played down or ignored, so that many women now judge male behaviour in terms of their own responses and emotions. And another consequence of the women's movement is that the conflict is now fought from a more sophisticated platform. Divorce is hardly to be considered a shameful consequence; and the much-vaunted equality of the sexes has simply given more license to the male aptitude for promiscuity. There was a time when the attacker was condemned by society, but that time is long past. Now, in these liberated days, wives of all ages are learning to perceive the Other Woman as one of the many hazards of living, like mugging or redundancy.

It seems to me that most women need a regular man in their lives, that most would prefer to have a husband. It occurs to me that the strangest thing of all is that this needs to be said. A striking number of both wives and Other Women said that they had had at some time or another a deep-seated fear that their husband or lover might leave them for another woman. It was a fear, often enough, that was entirely unrelated to their past or present circumstances.

This is why the Woman versus Woman conflict is relevant to almost everyone – to the girls of 18 who become the Other Woman, to the bewildered married man who suddenly finds himself discarding one family and starting another, to the wife who faces the potential destruction of her family and her innermost core.

The centre of the conflict is, of course, the man, who for the purposes of this book will be referred to as the husband. The husband is the prize. Or is he? My research shows that it is not uncommon for the married man to become relevant as a symbol only, a symbol of victory or a symbol of defeat. But whatever his ultimate role may be, his motivations, vulnerabilities, expectations, needs, attitudes and behavioural patterns are closely examined.

When a man fights another man over the same woman, more often than not his behaviour is direct and open. Ask him what he would do about the Other Man and he will lean forward in his chair, openly hostile, pugilistic, and, whatever his size, offer some sort of physical solution. It is highly unlikely that he will be concerned with the intricacies of his rival's personality. Ask a woman what she would do about the Other Woman and she will lean back, cross her legs, join her hands and consider. And this is how she is likely to behave whether or not it is because she has been conditioned to disguise her aggression. Differences in conduct in this area are such that there is no parallel to the Woman versus Woman conflict in the behaviour of men.

If very little is known of the battle, still less is known of the solitary, secret life of the Other Woman and how her numbers have multiplied. Neither accepted nor condemned, society accords her no place at all. For the Other Woman has an aura instead of a status. She is thought to be sexy, young and a miracle in bed, and yet she may be none of these. And whether or not she successfully fulfils her ambition and becomes a wife, if that indeed be her ambition, the Other Woman courts and causes more misery and more unhappiness to herself and to others than ever before.

Wedded as she is to being ready and available whenever her married man is free to see her, the Other Woman's life is secret and her loneliness private. Many endure this for years, tolerated, placeless souls living on fantasy, because from fantasy hope can be squeezed. Somehow, some day, some way, they fantasize, their married man's wife will simply vanish. Or he will divorce her – even though he declared, from the outset, that he would never do so. The secrecy which governs their lives is probably why they are unaware of how many share their condition. In the United States there are now clubs for Other Women, and organizations called Mistresses Anonymous and The Other Women's Bureau. Even so, the Other Woman may not be aware that she is not the only one who has not once dared to telephone her married man's home, not once in fifteen years; or that there are Other Women whose only satisfaction is that when their married man is with them, he is not with his wife; or that many husbands, after divorce from or even the death of their wives, do not marry their long-standing Other Women; nor do they know anything of the astonishing frequency with which their abortion results in a new baby for their married man's wife. It would seem that it is that very secrecy, so gloriously essential at the beginning of the relationship, that finally undermines – and, in a sense, entombs – the Other Woman.

But some Other Women are so dedicated and absorbed by their own careers that they find that a steady relationship with one man, once-weekly or once-fortnightly, is enough to satisfy that urge that won't go away – to have one basic, regular, if extraneous man in their lives. They have the security that goes with a stable relationship, while still preserving the bliss of freedom without commitment. Even so, most Other Women so far interviewed longed to marry, or at least live with, their married man.

Many women who defer marriage in favour of their own careers find that when they are ready for motherhood and marriage an insufficient number of unmarried men, compatible or otherwise, are available to them. Many men reacted to the women's movement by proclaiming themselves ineligible for marriage; Erica Jong observed that women lost more men to male homosexuality than were lost in two world wars.

A recent study (*Too Many Women?* by Marcia Guttentag

and Paul F. Secord, Sage, 1983) has shown that between 1960 and 1990 women reaching the age of 33 or older have far fewer opportunities for marriage. In 1980, for every 100 women aged between 33 and 37 there were only eight-four men. Given that, on average, most men marry women two years younger than themselves, a scarcity of marriageable men must be of some relevance to the rise in the number of Other Women.

To place the Other Woman's position in any sort of realistic perspective, we ought at least to consider the following: *the chances of being under the threat of the Other Woman are only marginally greater than the chances of becoming the Other Woman.* The Other Woman who is already married is far from a rarity. The wife who dissolves her marriage in order to marry someone else's husband frequently finds herself husbandless, assuming the grim, grey mantle of the Other Woman, subjecting herself and even her children to its accompanying torment.

The panicky, hysterical reaction of the wife to the Other Woman destroys more marriages than the Other Woman herself. Those wives who understood that they were the casualties of their husband's helpless ecstasy rather than the victim of his deliberate cruelty not only prevented unnecessary divorces but, contrary to their own and others' expectations, gained immeasurably in self-respect and in a number of instances the marriage was made stronger. They saw the Other Woman as a challenge instead of a humiliation. The same is true of those wives who did not panic, but all the same fell to the Other Woman, if only because they perceived the Other Woman as one of the many hazards of present-day living.

The conventional wisdom, held by marriage counsellors and other such 'experts', that the Other Woman is invariably the consequence and never the cause of a failing marriage accounts for numerous unnecessary divorces. This myth also compounds the crisis of confidence, the self-blame (she begins to believe she deserved to lose her husband) and the heartbreak experienced by the displaced wife. (Small wonder, therefore, that at the time of writing no study in the UK has yet evaluated the efficacy of the marriage counsellor.)

There are many excellent reasons for divorce, but the Other Woman or, for that matter, the Other Man, need not be one of them. Yet too many wives believe that the very existence of the Other Woman means that the marriage has ended, the family destroyed. The same is true of the Other Woman who thinks that her very existence means that if the marriage is not already in a serious state of dissolution, it soon will be.

Woman versus Woman, with its many stories from both inside and outside marriage, explodes these myths by examining in depth this two-sided conflict and three-sided entanglement which has baffled, intrigued and involved men and women everywhere for centuries.

1

Permanent inquests

Most people seem to find it extraordinarily difficult to accept that a husband would leave his wife and children because he prefers someone else, and for no other reason. It is too frightening and too threatening to accept that anything so trivial as preference would be permitted to cause the destruction of a family. Such a preference has to be explained and justified, and usually at the expense of the wife.

Therefore when a man leaves his wife, it is not mere preference, it is *unavoidable* preference. A happily married man would not have fallen in love with the Other Woman unless his wife had tripped him. The prevailing wisdom has it that no one ever leaves a happy marriage for someone else; *it is taken for granted that the defection is in itself evidence and proof that the marriage was a failure.* It is not that people no longer regard marriage as important, rather it is that the marital relationship is of such overwhelming importance that they choose to believe that it must be deeply flawed indeed for it to break. It is as if there is a terrible reluctance to accept or to come to terms with the fact that the Other Woman can turn an ordinary healthy family, with ordinary healthy problems, in other words, a family whole in every sense, into one that is broken and sick. Far more attention is devoted to broken families than to those whose survival is allowed to rest in the hands of the Other Woman, or, again, the Other Man. *If the causes and consequences of the Other Woman were better known and recognized, and received more coverage, there might well be fewer divorces, as well as fewer Other Women.*

A broken marriage poses a threat even to supposedly 'ideal' unions. It is, in part, the fear of contamination that prompts a rapid condemnation of the stricken wife.

'She let herself go.'
'She was forever on a diet.'
'She gave more attention to her job than to him.'
'She always tried to compete with him.'
'She was a bad mother.'
'She was obsessive about her kids.'
'She drank too much.'
'She wouldn't even take a glass of wine.'
'She was a slut.'
'She was a compulsive housekeeper.'

Other married women, therefore, often prefer to avoid the losing wife, though only after the novelty or excitement has worn off. And then, driven to diminish the threat still further, they turn the losing wife into a scapegoat: 'She brought it on herself', and she is blamed for having done so. It is not that they are driven by malice, rather it is more in the nature of protection – a defence mechanism that seeks to deny the innateness of the male aptitude for promiscuity.

Faced with the Other Woman, far too many wives assume too much of the blame. Some are paralysed by it and never forgive themselves, others overcome it, and a few – far too few – are not prone to it. The handling of that inner conflict is one of the primary battlefronts of the Woman versus Woman conflict.

Misguided guilt is even more destructive than misguided faith and, blinded by self-blame, many a wife accepts that the loss (or potential loss) of her husband to the Other Woman is her fault, and no more than she deserves. She assumes this guilt the way she has allocated it to other similarly afflicted wives in the past. . . . Tradition, culture and biology all play a part in the tendency of a wife to blame herself. But whether or not it is because women have been taught (since biblical times) to believe that 'home is the wife', the deserted wife feels that she has failed at the most crucial of all her concerns, the survival of her family. Motherhood increases a woman's awareness of personal responsibility; the fear of failing a child is as strong as the will to protect it. Parenthood implies responsibility, but most mothers claim the ultimate responsibility for the wellbeing of the child. The awesomeness with which women weigh this responsibility has some connection to this tendency to assume the blame. Her husband has left, or is about to leave. Accordingly, she feels that she has not only let herself down but also her children and, paradoxical as it may seem, even her husband. 'What did I do that was so wrong that it made him do this to himself?'

To assume blame is to hold oneself accountable for both the cause and the consequences of the disaster. It is a way of compounding the disaster. 'I should have known he was not happy with me' is the constant echo in the brain and heart. She panics, and rages against herself. She rages against herself and panics. Where she does not lapse into a paralysis of despair, she lapses into hysteria. She shrieks, she raves, she rants; she becomes the Other Woman's greatest ally. The more abuse she pours on the Other Woman's head, the more support she gives her. She knows this, sometimes, but cannot stop. Ironically, the self-blame persists long after the surrender. 'I shouldn't have let myself go to pieces like that,' said Mary, aged 40, mother of four, and a nurse. She had been unable to stop herself from crying, her face was always 'swollen and blotchy', she lost her temper and threw an ashtray at him, and it shattered against his forehead. She'd thought they had a 'wonderful marriage, everyone thought so, too'. The fact that Mary couldn't begin to guess what 'he saw in *her*' (the Other Woman was 48, four years older than he, and 'looked like hell') made things worse. It diminished

Mary in her own eyes. She feels now that she 'should have tried to help him get over it'.

Mary is fairly typical of all those wives whose panicky, hysterical reaction makes their defeat all the more certain.

Even if in the end mental breakdown or near derangement is escaped, cataclysmic disequilibrium is common. Breakdown as a response to the Other Woman is not uncommon. Even when it is a subconscious weapon of retaliation in the Woman versus Woman conflict it tends to rebound. Her nervous breakdown or suicide attempt is, says the Other Woman, 'only an excuse to keep you!'.

Typical of the tendency towards self-blame is Audrey. At 43 Audrey is attractive, humorous and competent. She has four children ranging in age from 12 to 18. Audrey's husband Eddie, a sales manager aged 50, left her for her best friend. Audrey and Francine had been close since they were both 10. Audrey now blames herself because she not only failed to recognize the early warning signals, but because she refused to see them. Audrey now also blames herself for having enjoyed a deep and sisterly relationship with Francine in the first place. Each woman knew everything about the other; they shared in the upbringing of their children and comforted each other through their children's serious illnesses. They shared their most intimate thoughts, hopes, grievances and joys, and 'lived in one another's pockets'. Once, fifteen years earlier, Audrey had thought that Francine and Eddie had danced too closely, but when she had remarked on it 'they laughed, and told me I was mad. I laughed with them!'

When Francine's husband was killed in a car crash three years ago, they were all inconsolable. Of course Eddie helped Francine sort out her financial affairs after that, and Audrey was proud of her husband's kindness. How cuttingly her mother's warnings – 'If you don't watch Francine you'll have only yourself to blame!' – now legitimize her self-accusation.

One evening, after Eddie had been helping Francine with her late husband's insurance policy, they all met for coffee and that was 'how I was told the truth about my husband and my best friend. It was then that Francine, with whom I had shared all, reminded me of a fleeting infidelity eighteen years before – the man in question must have forgotten all about it too.'

The double betrayal by a friend does nothing to alleviate self-blame. She details all the signals she was 'too blind, too stupid and too confident to see'. She searches in her mind for her earliest remembrances of her relationship with Francine. She had never seen her as anything like a competitor, because she now thinks she must have always felt superior. Here there is more reason for self-blame, compounded by not having understood how much Francine may have needed to hurt her. She is convinced it was her poor judgement that caused the destruction of what had once been a humorous, happy family with the usual ups and downs.

Audrey, like many deserted wives, is engaged in a permanent inquest. Although she concedes that both Eddie and Francine are not without guilt, her major finding is that she failed to keep her man.

'She couldn't keep her man' is so common a statement that it is almost a cliché. One hardly ever hears 'he couldn't keep his wife.' It's hard to imagine a man whose best friend runs off with his wife blaming himself for his poor judgement in having chosen such a friend. Countless articles on the theme of how to keep your man appear regularly in newspapers and magazines, but how many articles are there on how to keep your woman? The loss of a man to the Other Woman, then, is a matter that concerns and preoccupies women far more than men. Indeed, emotional relationships are the motor force inside most of their lives.

Another example of this willingness to take the blame is illustrated by Brenda Maddox in her excellent book *Married and Gay*. Writing of the experience of a wife finding out that her husband is involved with another man, she states:

'It says something about the male misunderstanding of women that gay husbands totally mistake what the reaction of their wives will be when told; it is not rage, not 'Out you filthy queer!' but rather 'What is wrong with *me*?' So that even when the husband's involvement is not with the Other Woman, but with another man, and due to factors altogether beyond the marital relationship, the wife still blames herself. And, interestingly enough, some of these wives chose to stay married. Many homosexual men 'stressed how sexually satisfied their wives were . . . and also how stoically the women had borne the occasional venereal disease that came their way.'

Ellen and Simon Thompson had been married for twenty years. Both were physicians, both were dedicated to their three children, themselves all-round high-achievers. In short, they were the perfect couple, the perfect family, to themselves and to everyone who knew them. Ellen was noted for her calm intelligence, her incisive wisdom and her realistic attitudes. But when she found out about Nancy who was older and far less attractive than she was, all her intelligence, calm and wisdom absconded. She lapsed into panic, hysteria and self-blame. The marriage ended in divorce, with Simon entirely estranged from the children to whom he had been so devoted.

During the twenty years of their marriage, the Thompsons had combined their image of the world at large, and disliked and admired the same things. They and their children played the piano and the violin to near concert standard. Together they supervised their children's class projects. The family curriculum included tennis in the summer and skiing in the winter. Household chores were shared. They were trilingual, in English, French and German, and different days of the week were allocated to different languages. Both Ellen and Simon worked and finances were never a problem. They were in complete agreement as to the distribution of their combined income – which meant that piano lessons took priority over clothing. Neither were afraid of the evidence of love, both were openly and spontaneously affectionate. In company they projected a united image of confidence that did not fall far short of arrogance. Since they were both physicians, it seemed both logical and right that their one surviving parent, Simon's ailing father, should come to live with them. The 'correct medical philosophy' as Simon put it, was to have an aged parent die in the bosom of the family and not in an impersonal, sterile home for the elderly. They both missed his father, whose classically peaceful death conformed to their ideals.

Ellen was first alerted to the existence of the Other Woman when she saw two airline tickets left, with apparent carelessness, on the bedroom chest of drawers. Medical conferences and meetings obliged Simon to travel abroad. One of the tickets was made out to Nancy, a scientist who worked with Simon. Nancy was eight years older than Simon, and so unattractive that, but for two factors, Ellen would have dismissed any possibility of Nancy being any sort of rival at all. The first and very obvious point was that Simon had not mentioned that Nancy would be accompanying him. But the second point was rather more obscure. Ellen's sudden recollection of the moment she had first met Nancy flooded through her with alarming force. She recalled exactly where Nancy had been standing – near the lift – when they first met, about two years earlier. She also recalled what she subsequently described as an 'intuition of threat'. But she had banished all this from her mind, and during those two years had helped Simon write Nancy's progress reports.

When she saw those two tickets, her intuition told her to say nothing. But Simon was hardly through the front door when she confronted him with the tickets and launched into an inquisition. She could not stop herself even though she knew that Simon had intended her to see the tickets he had laid out so conspicuously. At first Simon made a minor attempt to deny everything, but after about five minutes confessed that he and Nancy had been seriously involved for four months.

In the weeks that followed Ellen lapsed into rage, grief and hysteria. She behaved, she says, like an 'ignorant fishwife'. She threw things, she screamed, she wept, she blamed herself. Simon assured her that Nancy was a consequence and not a cause. He felt Ellen had been 'insensitive to his needs'; she ought not to have allowed him to suffer the stress and torment of his father's lengthy terminal illness. It was this final injustice, as much as sexual jealousy (Simon felt it would be disloyal to Nancy to sleep with Ellen) that altogether undid her. She was aware that Simon was under Nancy's influence, but she could not abide having what she saw as one of her strengths turned into a weakness. It had not been easy, the nursing of an incontinent, elderly, cantankerous man. . . . And now her effort was being turned against her.

She was beginning to blame herself for the hysterical violent scenes, for having seen the tickets, and worse still, for having confronted Simon with them. She began to believe she was making Simon feel guilty and blamed herself for having done so. She had already admitted to Simon that she had indeed expected and demanded too much from him with regard to their children's education. She began to blame herself for her involvement with their children. Simon now thought that they had spoiled their children with material things. Nancy's children had received scholarships, had taken paper rounds, vacation jobs and so on. Besides, Ellen had a small legacy – why hadn't she thought of using that money to buy a second car? But that thought had not crossed her mind; the money had been put aside for the children, for later. She had taken Simon's agreement for granted: it had never been discussed. That this had conformed with Simon's notion of how things should be done now seemed irrelevant. It was clear that she had taken Simon for granted, too, and she blamed herself accordingly.

A sanctimonious man of high moral integrity, Simon had

despised those of their friends and colleagues who went in for extramarital sex. He had always given of his best to all his professional, family and social obligations. His affair with Nancy went counter to all his values, and his attitude towards his family changed. Ellen therefore believed that his behaviour was being influenced by his terrible sense of guilt. She reasoned she could ease this by assuming most of the blame for Simon's actions. She went further: in an attempt to redress or at least equalize the balance of Simon's guilt, she confessed to an affair she had not had. It was by way of offloading his guilt that Ellen hoped to imply that she and her husband were even, that he was no worse than she. Later it rebounded. Ellen's alleged confession was conveyed to Nancy, and believed. Ellen is uncertain, now, whether or not she had hoped to make Simon jealous. She had always known that men and women react differently to jealousy, but had judged Simon to be more sophisticated than most and accordingly 'beyond such normal male reactions'.

Ellen told no one of their problems. The story only broke after Simon had left to set up house with Nancy. Most of Ellen's friends, when they heard about it, agreed not only that she had begun to let herself go, but that she had been too absorbed in her career, and one or two suggested to her that perhaps she had been competing with Simon as well?

This censorious attitude on the part of friends is not uncommon, as we have already seen. Ellen's aptitude for self-blame is not uncommon, either. Six years later, Ellen continues to blame herself for not having recognized that the 'basic marriage was at fault', even though she cannot pinpoint where or what had gone wrong. She feels she ought to have consulted Simon about her small legacy. She has added to her litany of self-blame by accusing herself of having concentrated on herself, on her hurt, on her suffering, when she should have based all her thinking and all her actions on the welfare of the family at large. She is convinced now that if only she had been less selfish she would not have allowed panic and hysteria to set in and overwhelm her.

At the time of Simon's defection the children had been in their teens. Their father insists that their mother has poisoned their minds against him. He refuses to acknowledge that the children reacted according to the moral precepts that *both* their parents had been at pains to teach. The children could not bring themselves to have anything to do with Nancy – their father demanded that they both accept and respect her. But the children had revered their father to the point of worship and he, for his part, had accepted and perhaps even promoted their idolatry. The children could not go against the principles with which they had been so assiduously indoctrinated. Ellen did not urge her children to accept Nancy, nor did she encourage them to reject her. She blames herself now for having *caused* the continuing estrangement from their father. Simon's only communication with his former family is via lawyers.

It is worth mentioning that Simon was not the only married man within the department in which both he and Nancy worked with whom she had become seriously entangled. Nancy, however, did not leave her own husband until Simon moved out of his home and acquired a separate establishment.

Those women who surmount the tendency to assume the blame are those who are most likely to plan a strategy of defence. For, as noted earlier in this chapter, self-blame leads to panic and hysteria, and too often to a paralysis of will.

It was many years before Christine Maddison was able to conquer what she saw as her natural and proper inclination to take the blame for her husband's philandering. Her story is worth going into at some length. For the sudden and final realization that his love affairs were not her fault was the secret not only of her own survival, but of the survival of her marriage.

Theirs was the sort of marriage that warmed others; they spread their welcoming happiness about them like invigorating air. Tall and graceful, the Maddisons were a handsome couple. Christine was 23 and Stephen 33 when they married and from the very beginning they embraced both their extended families as they embraced each other. Stephen's parents had divorced when he was 11, and the parents, stepparents and in-laws were frequent visitors. They found comfort and encouragement at the Maddisons for the intensity of the young couple's devotion to one another was softened and made safe by Stephen's brand of irreverent humour. Both the Maddisons were born leaders, both were interested in the minutiae of other people's lives. If Stephen's business acumen appeared magical, the magic was supplied by the simplicity, bordering on innocence, of Christine's sure instincts. For Stephen was an innovative property developer, whose name, four years after his marriage, moved hardened bankers, city lawyers, stockbrokers and their ilk to unqualified admiration of such dimensions that they admired themselves for even having known him. Stephen saw Christine as his lucky talisman, and that was hardly surprising, for the blend of informality and elegance with which she entertained his associates, and handled his staff, made even a telephone encounter with her a memorable event. She knew about their lives, as they knew about hers. Three sons were born within the first three years of their marriage, the third following eleven months after the birth of twins.

It was soon after their ninth anniversary that Christine began to believe that Stephen and her best friend were closer than they ought to be. Stephen was the sort of man who flirted with everyone – with men as well as with women – for he had an almost uncanny way, as he stood talking with his glass in one hand, with his arm draped over his companion's shoulder, of making that person feel more than important, even valuable to him. He seemed to winkle out their secret hopes and dreams. Perhaps it was the irreverence of his sympathy, perhaps the soundness of his unshockability, perhaps the sheer force of his undoubted intelligence, or perhaps the combination of all of these, that left others feeling safely purged, rather than fearful, after having entrusted him with their deepest confidences.

Christine glowed in his presence, she managed to communicate her awareness of her sense of privilege, which was why those who might have begrudged her her happiness loved her instead. She neither tried nor wanted to compete with him or his flamboyance; and when his affair with her close friend, Joan, was followed by other affairs, she was one of those women whom other wives could not fault. They could not say (no matter how much they wished they could!) that she did not keep up with him, that she let herself go, that she was dull. But although others saw this, Christine did *not* – of course there must be something wrong with her, she was sure. She simply could not believe that Stephen would do this sort of thing to her if she did not deserve it. For, just as he made others believe that he loved them, so he made her believe it too: she despised herself even more for not being able to keep him for herself. She applied her female values to his behaviour; she did not realize the extent to which men differed from women, nor did she know that it was not only useless, but counterproductive to think that she would have died rather than hurt him as he hurt her.

Stephen tried to explain that she was his wife, and therefore sacred; he tried to assure her that he would never leave and went as far as to structure his finances to make this almost an economic impossibility. But Christine became lethargic, apathetic, preoccupied and vague. She longed to leave him, but loved him, and could not. She had lost her self-respect. The agonies and torments of her jealousies and fears reached poetic heights and lows – sleeplessness once compelled her to chew four strong barbiturates in a luckless effort to get enough sleep.

However, since we have dealt fairly extensively with the tendency of wives to accept the blame for the Other Woman, it would be useful to describe how Christine overcame this, and is now, by the way, an enlightened but unembittered survivor, able to enjoy her marriage and her sons, able to endure the flaws in her ever-deepening, if unconventional, relationship with Stephen. (It ought to be said here that she is one of those rare women for whom the trappings of her husband's success have not spelt contamination. She is a down-to-earth fundamentalist who likes to help others if she can, she makes and keeps friends regardless of their station.)

During the eleven years that it was widely known that Stephen had close associations with other women, Christine blamed herself. She took to driving her car aimlessly, for hours and hours. She would drive with no destination in mind; it was a symbol of what her marriage had become. Her despair, like her sense of failure, was boundless, for she had long since come to the conclusion that she did not love her husband but was obsessed by him; his every word, indeed his every syllable was weighed by her and assessed almost as if she had never heard him before, or, worse, might never hear him again.

On one of her aimless drives, she stopped her car beside a deserted tennis court, and, as usual, asked herself, *why, why, why*?

Why did Stephen do this to her?

And then it came to her like this: supposing that tennis court were filled with lovely women, lovely girls, girls and women of every shape, and every hue, each standing jammed one against the other, each with arms outstretched, hands raised supplicatingly, each saying, But I love you, Stephen, only *you*. You. You. It's only you I love, Stephen. Then Stephen would reply that it's not enough, it is still not enough.

And so Christine came at last to an understanding that the Other Women (and there have been several, one or two more important than the others) were not her fault. She has been an ardent campaigner in the Woman versus Woman conflict; in resisting the Other Women's humiliating invitations to direct confrontation she has used more discipline than she knew she had. But she now feels that even though the result might have been the same if she had known and understood and accepted, her suffering would not have been as acute, as destructive and as dangerous. Planning suicide had been her most important consolation. She has now been married for twenty-five years, and would like other wives who suffer similarly to have the benefit of her insight. That this insight should *not* have been so painfully arrived at goes without saying. One could argue that Christine's suffering was due to an individual neurosis, but this would lose sight of the frequency with which *wives as a group* tend to blame themselves for the Other Woman.

Thanks to the women's movement some modifications have been, and are being made, but the double standard is still with us, however unjust, however galling, and whether or not it owes its existence to history or to nature, the double standard also represents the differences between men and women. Sometimes one feels that the differences are too comprehensive to admit measurement, and perhaps it is only via a recognition of the extent of the differences that any sort of understanding between the sexes can be achieved. Of course there are people who will despise Christine's acceptance of what she sees as Stephen's weakness, and who will wonder, angrily, why she didn't send him to hell. But Christine now understands that it is harder for men not to be promiscuous than it is for women not to be promiscuous. She also understands that a glimpse of an anonymous pretty leg, or the sight of an anonymous female thigh, or the oblique view of an anonymous breast, the shape of an anonymous hip, can send a message to the penis in the way an anonymous strong shoulder, or an anonymous hairy chest, or an anonymous bicep can seldom send a message to the vagina. But it is the recognition or otherwise of this difference that is one of the major motors of the Woman versus Woman conflict. It is also one of the chief reasons why there is almost no parallel Man versus Man conflict.

Christine, for her part, feels that in preserving her family as well as her own integrity and her own identity, she has fulfilled herself and found her truest expression as a woman.

Christine is convinced that her integrity, like her identity, rests on not applying a woman's standards to a man. She says very simply that she is first a woman, and then a person. It would seem that, so far, fewer men than women have been required to make this distinction.

In 1959, in *The Province of the Heart*, Phyllis McGinley said, 'Women are not men's equals in anything except responsibility. We are not their inferiors, either, or even their superiors. We are quite simply different races.' These words are as relevant now as they were in 1959.

2

Jealousy's consuming passion

It is a rare individual who has the luxury of freedom from jealousy's consuming passion. And while jealousy intrudes in our lives from the earliest pangs of sibling rivalry, nowhere does it assume the shattering dimensions seen in the Woman versus Woman conflict.

Suspicion, a state of uncertainty and doubt that precedes jealousy, unleashes all manner of known and new emotions. The interval between suspicion and its proof is felt by many wives to have been even more painful than its confirmation.

Many wives, during the period of unconfirmed but relentless suspicion, begin to doubt not only their husbands but also their own sanity. The fear of losing their husbands is compounded by the fear of losing their minds. Proof of the existence of the Other Woman may at least be proof of their own sanity. Thus many wives find themselves in an unresolvable dilemma; confirmation, for some, means 'cold relief'. Hoping their suspicions are ill-founded, many would almost rather be wrong and crazy than right and sane. Hoping for reassurance they often confide their secret suspicions to their husbands, who defensively accuse them of 'being mad'. Thus they may be reassured, yet, if the suspicions persist, terrified of madness. Sometimes this fear of madness is powerful enough to force a wife to put the suspicion from her mind, leading later to the self-reproach of 'how could I have been so blind?'

It is during this uncertain phase that wives find themselves confronting hidden fears. Is she so neurotic that she is 'putting it all on her husband'? Still, something seems to be wrong, perhaps it's her fault. . . . The awareness of some ill-defined problem does not necessarily lead a wife to conclude at once that there must be another woman. However, the uncertainty that characterizes suspicion is in itself enough to shatter self-confidence and with it self-respect.

At 39, Jennifer, a tall woman of imposing beauty, was told by her husband, Peter, that her suspicions were evidence that she was 'going senile'. Jennifer was not by nature a suspicious person; her honesty, implanted by a thorough and extensive New England education, assumed that all those who were close to her were similarly honest. Her suspicions, therefore, so alien, so primitive, struck at the heartland of her being that took other people's honour for granted. But her suspicions were firmly based. For at 44 Peter had become excessively vain; he took to colouring his hair, to wearing pink shirts, to subtly elevated shoes to enhance his height even though he was taller than most.

It had been a happy marriage for nineteen years. An international industrialist, Peter's work often took him away, and when he phoned, Jennifer would tell him to come back quickly. And sometimes he would interrupt a trip and return for a night. He was a successful businessman, successful father, the loved and respected, even revered chairman of the family.

Jennifer, involved with and fulfilled by her family commitments, continued with the painting and illustration she had so ardently studied. She held exhibitions, her talent was acknowledged and her husband, who knew he came first, was proud and encouraging.

His sudden preoccupation with his physical appearance coincided with bizarre changes in his behaviour. He would leave the house, sneakily go away to a boat show that turned out to be entirely fictitious (Jennifer found out not by snooping, but by chance), and the hotel names on newspapers he brought back turned out to be other than the hotels he had claimed to have stayed at. Again, Jennifer asked what was wrong, and again Peter told her that she ought to 'keep herself busier' (but she was so busy), 'not to concentrate so much on him' (but he was her husband), and that she was getting senile, ought to see a doctor (but she was in the rudest health). It was *her* madness, *her* imagination, *her* sick mind that was wrong, it was nothing else. She had become a crazy woman, he said, hell-bent on destroying everything! And Peter, who had been uncritical, criticized her; at dinner he would tell the children not to listen to their mother, she talked nonsense and didn't even know what she was talking about. His criticism, over several months, became a daily event. Dazed, Jennifer heard that she was inefficient, disorganized, that she could never do anything right any more. Even her taste was called into question. Peter had been the undisputed chairman of the family, Jennifer's role had been managing director. She felt herself being demoted, displaced, and doubted her sanity and doubted all her perceptions of everything.

Yet Peter was not a cruel man, nor was he irrational. Indeed, in their circles, the acuity of his logic, like his business acumen, was, in a minor way, legendary. He was a wise man, steeped in knowledge of the arts, of Eastern religions; a travelled, sophisticated blend of the dedicated, and often necessarily ruthless negotiator who was ready to give advice and, sometimes, money, though only if he thought it would help. Peter respected Jennifer's perceptions of human behaviour just as he respected and welcomed her acknowledgement that she would always be something of a stranger to the commercial world. Something in her own behaviour, then, must have led Peter to conclude that her mind was sick, that her imagination was evil, that she was going mad, and, since it was clear that things were going wrong, it was clear that it was her mind that was at fault.

She always unpacked his suitcases and aired his clothes when he came back. Once she found a tube of mascara and, when she asked what it was doing there, he said that he used it to conceal the roots of his grey hairs, and pointed out, reasonably, that looking youthful was necessary to his business. She accepted that. She did not want to appear crazy any more than she wanted to be crazy. The terror of going mad made her hold herself physically rigid, as if a straight back would somehow ensure a straight mind. So she wore her fear of madness like a corset. She knew, very well, that people did go mad, suddenly, but there was no history of insanity in her family – or was there? Another time, she lifted one of his jackets, and it weighed her arm down, heavy as a sculpture. She looked in the pockets to find a collection of gold bracelets, necklaces, earrings. She asked about them, and was told that he had decided to invest in gold, because surely even Jennifer knew gold had risen by twenty dollars that very week? Jennifer did not know, and accordingly said nothing.

Meanwhile, Peter took to locking the door of his study when he went away. The filing cabinet and desk drawers had always been locked, which was natural enough, but never the door. It occurred to Jennifer that Peter was locking his study as if it were Pandora's box. The third time he went away and locked the study she searched for and found a duplicate key. It didn't take long, perhaps five minutes, before she had uncovered his American Express receipts, one of which was for two first-class tickets; she read carefully, strangely conscious of the grace of the handwriting, in the space beside 'relation of passenger to cardholder', the word 'fiancée'. That word spelled, as she says now, absolute positive proof that she was not mad, and she felt a relief that bordered on euphoria. She was aware, even at that moment, of having accomplished a great deal, of having reached a crucial milestone, of having found out something terribly important about herself.

During the period when the identity of the adversary is unknown, suspicion is a torment. Wracked with jealousy and often consumed by morbid curiosity, most wives believe that the Other Woman has the advantage in two areas. First, the Other Woman knows that her adversary is real and not only a suspicion, which means *she* is not haunted by the spectre of going mad. Second, the Other Woman is able to make a fairly shrewd assessment of her enemy's strengths and weaknesses. (This does not take into account the woman who is unaware that she is the Other Woman because she does not know that the man is married.)

It is during this phase that a wife has to decide whether or not to go to war, to decide whether she is threatened. At this stage her enemy is as mysterious as she is invisible. Yet she senses that she and her family are under attack and that she must embark either on a passive or active defence. She may be compelled to resort to subterfuge, sensitive to the dangers of letting her husband know of her suspicions. The survival instinct turns her into a spy. She believes, understandably, that she cannot gauge either the quality of the threat, or the degree of danger, unless she is able to confirm her suspicions and ultimately the identity of her enemy.

As Leslie Farber says in his splendid essay, 'Jealousy', 'What sets jealousy apart from other possible responses to a real or imagined infidelity – such as rage and grief – is its quality of obsession. . . . Literally, obsession means being oppressed or besieged, as if by an evil spirit'. Confirming the existence and unearthing the identity of the Other Woman, then, becomes the focus of the obsession. Yet the actions taken by an assailed wife, however innovative, however constructive in intent, are frequently viewed by society as idle curiosity at best or malicious troublemaking at worst. Of course her actions and investigations may be motivated in part by a curiosity of the most powerful and terrible kind, but it is too often forgotten that the magnitude of the threat posed by the Other Woman actively engages both the survival and the maternal instincts. The obsession is rooted in these two commanding instincts, and then fertilized by the terrors of rejection.

This obsessive *need* to confirm and identify the Other Woman is a tremendous stimulus to the imagination. The will to know supersedes everything, and no effort is, or can be, too great.

Surely it was more than curiosity which led Claire to look through every single page of the telephone directory until she reached L and found the name and the address that matched the number she sought?

Few leads are too flimsy to follow. The search proceeds with all the fervour and all the patience of a mighty obsession. Motor cars are searched, letters or addresses or photographs are found. Mary discovered a latchkey concealed under the carpet of a boat, but though it was numbered she did not succeed, for all her efforts, in tracing the lock. Jean discovered a letter in the glove compartment. Wives, as the search continues, become burglars. Brief-cases and offices are broken into and desks are searched. Wives become detectives, disguise specialists, wigs and other related objects are pressed into action. Some have gone to the lengths of hiring a car to follow their husbands. Those who can afford it, and often those who can't, engage private detectives.

Photographs are examined with a magnifying glass, handwriting is subjected to the analysis of a graphologist. In the course of such an obsession the services of astrologers and clairvoyants are called upon. Besides the conventional methods of mail interception such as opening envelopes by steam, a passport may be taken to Poste Restante just in case there might be a letter to claim. Some wives placed a 'bug' in the car, and one succeeded in getting a bug in the office – anything to clarify the doubt, ironically in the hope that the known will alleviate the fear and dispel the terror of jealousy.

For as long as the existence and identity of her rival remains a mystery the threatened wife is tortured by her own overworked, but far from worn-out, imagination. Her imagination tortures itself still further by questioning whether or not it is all only in the imagination anyway. Is she really going mad? Is there another woman? But who is the Other Woman? *Who is she*? And it is at this point that her imagination outdoes itself in its seemingly endless ability to inflict torture. The speculation is endless. Oh, of course, she is young and beautiful and sexy, and new and different: women in their twenties apply the same formula.

Walking down the street, at work, shopping or in the park she scans the faces, the bodies, the shape of every attractive woman she sees. Is *this* the one? She's sure she'll 'just be able to tell . . .'. No wonder the confirmation of her worst forebodings is sometimes a source of such exquisite relief.

It is during this uncertain phase that a wife begins to evaluate not only herself but also her marriage. If she is happy, she becomes uncertain about him. Is he unhappy? But even while both the existence and the identity of the Other Woman remains a mystery, the wife begins to look at herself and her own appearance. She may decide to change her appearance in some way; she may go on a diet, change her hairstyle, or acquire new underwear. More than one wife has resorted to plastic surgery.

Ruth knew that her husband Ben, a rather vain and shallow man, found her nose displeasing. His Other Woman, Fran, had a perfect nose. Ruth changed her nose, and Ben changed back to her.

Suspicion can be as potent an aphrodisiac as fame. Others become more imaginative in bed, or are more demanding and feel more sexy. Subconsciously, though still in doubt, she is already trying to fight back. Her attempt to please him is at the same time an attempt to minimize the advantages of the Other Woman. Sometimes it seems as if her mind has been occupied by a phantom; the unknown virtues and qualities of her mysterious rival are always with her, as palpable as a presence.

Before going on to consider the moment when the reality of the threat is established (whether or not the identity of the

Other Woman is known), it is necessary to examine the factors that led to the recognition of the threat in the first place. These factors, or early warning signals, are strikingly relevant to the Woman versus Woman conflict.

Female instinct is, of course, as central to the Woman versus Woman conflict as it is central to male/female relations. It is this instinct that promotes the belief that one way of winning a man from a rival is to outwit her. This instinct, and therefore the Woman versus Woman conflict, may owe its origins to the subconscious knowledge that men are more promiscuous than women. 'It is to the reproductive advantage of men to have casual sex with as many partners as possible . . . the conscious motives of the parties may be in direct opposition to the sexual instincts involved' (Glenn Wilson, *Love and Instinct*).

It is this instinctive awareness of the male aptitude for promiscuity that leads women to feel that their long-term, or important, sexual relationships are always at risk. Since this knowledge hardly makes for security, it is often pushed aside, if not repressed. But when the need arises the hidden knowledge surfaces.

Whether women evaluate most of their female friends and associates in terms of their potential threat quotient because of some residual but primitive unseen instinct, or simply as a conditioned response to the well-known male promiscuity factor, has yet to be determined. One hardly need say that some women are more in touch with their instincts than others. Meanwhile, suffice it to say that many a husband (at a social gathering or a party) has been nonplussed by his wife's unerring perception of the very woman he had found most sexually appealing, however unlikely or even surprising the candidate, to say nothing of how well he thought he had concealed his response.

It is the early warning signal, or symptom, that highlights those mild differences in behaviour that might otherwise have gone unobserved. While most of the early warning signals cited below are interesting, and even amusing, their significance lies in the rapid way in which wives not only concluded that their husband was involved with an Other Woman, but assessed the strength of his involvement, and therefore the strength of their rival, as well.

Oliver suddenly spent an awful lot of time manicuring his toenails. (Married seventeen years.)

Richard began dyeing the hair on his chest. (Married twenty-four years.)

Michael went in for a hair transplant. Although Michael was afraid of doctors, hospitals and anaesthetics, he went in for elective surgery. (Married twenty-seven years.)

Edward bought himself a sunlamp. (Married ten years.)

Paul bought a very trendy overcoat with a hood. His wife's 'immediate instinct' was that 'he'd got it bad for a very young girl'. (Married twenty years.)

Larry always wore striped ties. His wife had fallen into the habit of noting the direction of the stripe in his tie in the mornings. She realized his tie had been retied during the day. (Married thirty years.)

All his life Colin had taken three sugars in his hot drinks. He suddenly announced that he was not taking sugar anymore. (Married twelve years, now divorced.)

Gail watched her husband cross a room three times within two hours to take a cigarette from Pamela's pack. He had a full pack of his own in the back pocket of his jeans. She quickly and rightly concluded that things were very serious. (Married nine years.)

George suddenly went from one to two packs a day. His wife correctly guessed that he was involved with a heavy smoker. (Married sixteen years, now divorced.)

Judy found a box of matches, gold tipped, and from a restaurant that was not on his company's expense account. (Married nineteen years, now divorced.)

Nicholas, who did not read fiction, began to read novels.

His wife accurately deduced the depth of his involvement. (Married twenty-eight years.)

Mark and his wife used to read the astrology charts together. She saw him read a new sign, smile and say nothing. (Married six years.)

Howard began using American phrases like 'you'd better believe me', 'parenting', and 'pushing emotional buttons'. His wife concluded that the Other Woman was an American. (Married twenty-five years.)

Brian and Margaret were at a dreary dinner party. Other than the hosts neither of them knew anyone who was there. Margaret heard a very ordinary-looking girl remark that Brian was eating peanuts '*again*'. She concluded that he and the girl were close to one another. (Married fourteen years, now divorced.)

Victor became a Beethoven fanatic. His wife guessed the Other Woman was a music lover, and knew who she was. (Married eight years, now separated.)

Derek developed a sudden taste for TV comedies, which he had not liked. Nothing, but nothing could draw him away from *Soap*. 'What a switch in interests! If you knew him, you'd know what I mean. . . . He's the serious type, almost grim. . . . He was so defensive about it all that I simply had to look further.' (Married eleven years.)

Steven suddenly seemed to know a lot about female contraceptive devices. (Married twenty years.)

If the early warning signal is difficult for a wife to ignore, the physical evidence of the Other Woman's presence in her own home is infinitely *more* difficult to ignore. A wife might find an earring at the bottom of her bed, hair on her own hairbrush, her cosmetics rearranged in the bathroom, sometimes menstrual blood or semen on her own sheets. The Other Woman may have deliberately chosen to inform the wife of her existence. It is, after all, one way of throwing down the gauntlet. And, as far as the man is concerned, the hair on the brush was an accidental oversight. But many a wife refuses to acknowledge the evidence left for her information.

Despite its pungent odour, Helen made no mention of the rather large black lace bra she found among her own underwear. She laundered everything in that cupboard, however. Emma ignored the tampon floating in her toilet bowl. Alice washed her semen-soiled sheets.

The prosecution of the Woman versus Woman conflict continues even when one of the contestants refuses to acknowledge its existence. Indeed, silence and secrecy can be strikingly effective. For it is also a secret war of attrition well concealed from the man in the middle. The husband will not know of that earring at the bottom of the bed, or of those hairs on his wife's brush. One way of defeating planned mischief of this order is to refuse to acknowledge having seen it. Often the Other Woman finds that the temptation to leave some trace of her presence is overwhelming. Tess, aged 48, and a very successful lingerie buyer, knew her married man would never marry her. She did not, she said, want to 'make trouble' for him, and longed only to change the order of the bottles in the bathroom, but couldn't remember, now, whether she did or not. She thought she may have. . . .

Some Other Women have the idea that if the wife knew her husband was involved with another woman she would 'throw him out' or 'give him up' or 'ask for an immediate divorce' – and some wives do just that. The wife does not know because her husband is afraid 'of hurting her', or of 'breaking up his family'. If her married man is unwilling or unable to tell his wife, there must be some other way for her to know. Relaying the news to the wife, via indirect means, is a very common tactic. A letter or telephone call, often anonymous, informs the wife of something she ought to know. Another example of the same tactic is to transmit the intelligence through one of the wife's relations (a parent, an adult child, even a teenage child) or one of her friends. For some wives such a call is, as one described it, 'manna from heaven' and so she made the most of it; it was an easy way of getting out of the marriage. Some wives 'go to pieces' and a confrontation with the husband ensues. Others pretend the call never happened, the letter never received. The letter falls on blind eyes, the call on deaf ears.

Margaret, 32, married for eight years, was one of those who decided to 'take no notice' of the telephone call. She thought it wisest to 'avoid confrontation', in spite of the fact that the caller, who was, of course, 'telling her for her own good', informed her where she could actually see her husband with his girlfriend. When she told her 'friendly caller' that she didn't believe her, she was advised, for her own sake and because it was in her 'own best interests' to know what was 'going on', to go to a certain restaurant the next day where she would see 'what was going on' for herself. Margaret, however, did not go there 'to see for herself', but asked a discreet friend to do this for her.

Although the information was confirmed, Margaret said nothing to her husband. Instead, she concentrated on 'keeping the home fires burning'. Much later the woman who had made the call told Margaret's husband about it. When he questioned his wife, she admitted that she had received such a call but of course she hadn't believed a word of it, and then, because it would have been unnatural not to, she was compelled to ask him how *he* knew about it. He made the excuse that this sort of thing had been happening to 'a lot of the chaps at the office'.

Another wife told the caller that of course she knew about the affair, she always knew, 'he *always* tells me'. She suggested that the caller tell the 'poor girl she's only one of many'.

Jennifer, 48, married for twenty-five years, thought that her anonymous caller sounded very young and very nervous. She thanked her for the call, agreed that it was for her own good, but there were one or two things she thought the caller's friend ought to know, for her own good. He'd had lots and lots of girlfriends, and always would. His idea of fidelity, she said, was to be faithful to 'three or more women at the same time'.

Affairs require secrecy and encourage speculation and both of these heighten romance. (One is almost tempted to say that without sex or secrecy and speculation, there would be no romance.) Who knows about the two of them? Who could have guessed? How difficult it is not to 'give oneself away'! What if something showed, and all was discovered? Does his wife know? Does her husband? Do you think she has any idea? How can you be certain? If an affair is a kissing game, it is also a guessing game. The wife who knows but says nothing hopes to 'keep them guessing'. For example, a wife, having just made the acquaintance of the Other Woman in her husband's life and never letting on that she has the faintest clue about the relationship, might drop a seemingly careless observation about her husband, such as 'Oh, Tom's just like my husband, charming in company, difficult at home.' Such a wife hardly intends to supply more magic to their speculation. But if the Other Woman is married, it can, and often does, frighten her off. For who knows, 'perhaps his wife intends to tell my husband'.

Centuries of sanctioned male promiscuity have meant that the only recognized form of adultery was female adultery. The emphasis was on the male attitude towards it. The fact that the practice of male promiscuity was not only licensed, but an important measure of manhood, is not without relevance to the Woman versus Woman conflict. If it is true that many men want variety while women want stability, then it is perhaps also true that despite all effort to the contrary, women have always had as much, if not more, to fear from their own sex, than from the opposite sex. One of the consequences of this is that the attitude towards male sexual jealousy is very different from the attitude towards female sexual jealousy. Men are more likely to fasten on the sexual act whereas women look beyond it. This means that the implicit threat has different constructions for women than for men. A man's virility is involved, and his concern for his virility has, by virtue of its physiology, been of far more concern to him than femininity has ever been for a woman. Indeed, there is no female linguistic equivalent to virility. Since virility is not a factor that a woman has to concern herself with as part of her own anatomy, she is far more likely to project her jealousy into fear for the future. Although her sexual prowess may be in question, she is far more concerned, in this respect, with consequences than with causes. Therefore it is better to blame herself or the Other Woman than to blame her husband; as long as the Other Woman is not his fault there is room for hope. Some people hold that women are far more forgiving than men; a woman will forgive her wayward husband far more readily than she will the Other Woman. On this point, this is a sidelight: the wife finds it infinitely easier to forgive the Other Woman *after* she has been displaced by another rival.

3

Crisis of ecstasy, crisis of pain

The husband who contemplates leaving home for the Other Woman is in a crisis of ecstasy. If his wife knows, or even suspects, that his life is being given over to the Other Woman, she is in a crisis of pain. Therefore, though their crises are at opposite ends of the emotional spectrum, the husband and wife have a crisis in common. In these circumstances, then, *a wife becomes the unwitting casualty of her husband's ecstasy*. Paradoxically, however, the fact that his wife and family are casualties of his ecstasy adds to its heights and, what is more, validates it further. It is this validated ecstasy that effectively triggers the husband into actually leaving.

Such validated ecstasy precipitates all manner of changes in behaviour. He is in ecstasy because he is in love, which is why he is driven to perpetuate strange and bewildering cruelties.

Since his wife is both an additive and an obstacle to his ecstasy, she is also responsible for its consequences. Few wives are able to recognize ecstasy's role – terror and grief and jealousy have never made for rational thinking – instead (however understandably) they see themselves as victims of men, or of the Other Woman, or of cruelty, or of all of these, and seldom, very seldom, as the casualty of ecstasy. It is as if *his* ecstasy drives rational thought from his wife's mind just as surely as it has been driven from his.

Some wives contend that rational thinking at a time like this goes against all their established values; it smacks of calculating, ruthless, bloodless, heartless behaviour and more properly belongs to the Other Woman than to them. They give up, accordingly, never acknowledging that they could be casualties of ecstasy, steadfastly maintaining that they are victims of the Other Woman. That the Other Woman is the source of the ecstasy is somehow irrelevant. Besides, they see the recognition of the effects of ecstasy as a betrayal most commonly concerned with their understanding of romantic love. An unromantic, cold-blooded fight is very firmly excluded from their version of romantic love. It is these wives, women of high principle and even higher moral indignation, either liberated or unliberated, but essentially naive, who have forgotten, or never knew, or have been conditioned away from the concept of countering irrationality with cold rationality. Besides, it is somehow unvirtuous or unladylike or anti-feminist to apply strength and reason to heartbreak. A feminist may walk away in disgust, and leave the Woman versus Woman conflict to the shamefully unenlightened, a lady may resort to hysteria, tears, grief and its concomitant paralysis of thought, but a sensible woman knows that the Woman versus Woman conflict is older than recorded history, and that wars fought without the benefit of clear thinking are inevitably lost wars. Lapsing into *uncontrolled* hysteria is guaranteed to result in defeat; *controlled* hysteria, however, is rather different.

The belief that ecstasy cannot and should not be fought because it is demeaning and degrading to fight against someone else's ecstasy is responsible for countless unnecessary divorces. Certain developments in certain areas are making gender equality a reality, but certain exclusive gender characteristics are destined to be with us for ever. At any rate, much of the art and artifice of the Woman versus Woman conflict has been lost, partly as a result of women's liberation, but even more because of the illusions of romantic love. For example, a wife in her forties, refusing to acknowledge, accept or recognize the ecstasy brought on by an 18-year-old rival, gives up – how can she compete with an 18-year-old? But ecstasy has an unbroken record of burning itself out and it is to ecstasy that such a wife, if she wishes to remain married, must address herself.

However, without an understanding of ecstasy, there is little chance of overcoming it. Ecstasy is defined in the Oxford English Dictionary as 'the state of being "beside oneself", thrown into a frenzy or a stupor, with anxiety, astonishment, fear or passion'. Shakespeare wrote of the blasts of ecstasy, and it ought to be obvious that no state of ecstasy can ever be remotely constant, let alone institutionalized. Ecstasy is by definition transient, its survival, even as a transient experience, is dependent on the moment. And an endless supply of moments of this sort leads not to infinity but to extinction.

It is bad enough that ecstasy burns itself out, but it need not also burn out a good or working marriage. However, for all those marriages that are burnt out by ecstasy, other more acceptable reasons are found, which leads us once again to indict the myth which holds that marriages that crumble under the weight of ecstasy do so because the foundation is weak.

In *Love and Will* Rollo May talks of

> a fact which has been known all through man's history, but which our own age has accomplished the remarkable feat of forgetting, namely, that sexual love has the power to propel human beings into situations which can destroy not only themselves but many other people at the same time.

The power of ecstasy or romantic love is well known, and revered, but if the self-destructive power of ecstasy, romantic love or sexual infatuation is not ignored, it is excused. All the world loves a lover, and wishes him well, too. But it is widely believed that the deserted wife who is unable to wish her husband well should at least have the grace to step aside, to become a willing casualty. She is far too seldom encouraged to fight the Other Woman.

Why is it that women are not advised to concentrate on seeing their husbands and their families through what, almost inevitably, is only temporary ecstasy, but to concentrate instead on the virtues of being alone, the virtues of independence? Even R. D. Laing, as reported in *The Sunday Times* in May 1982, stated that the family is the last sanctuary of refuge, and yet, instead of protecting an existing family those professionally engaged in the marital field speak of serial remarriage, creative divorce and the like, even though 50 per cent of all second marriages end in divorce.

And yet, despite all this, those women who aspire to preserve their families and their marriages are held in a fair amount of contempt: 'It is immoral to try to hold on to a man who doesn't want you!'; 'No one has the right to a whole extra life – let him go'; 'What about your pride, your self-respect? Let him go. He doesn't want you!'

If we accept the statistics from as far back as 1948, about half of all married men have intercourse with someone other than their wives at some time during their marriage, and if we accept the theory that men have always been unfaithful, why do we have so much difficulty in recognizing ecstasy of the aphrodisiacal sort as a cause for marital breakdown?

The following account given by Vera Foster is illustrative of the rationale behind a considered defence. Vera was 41, married, she believed happily, for twenty-one years, when her husband, Neil, 45, met Jane, 33, married for twelve years. Vera had never imagined that she could possibly be the sort of woman who would even dream of trying to hold on to a man who even hinted that he no longer wanted her. When she was faced with this situation she had four children ranging in age from 7 to 20. Her husband, Neil, was a successful architect, keen on tennis and jogging, and involved, one could almost say engrossed, in his family.

At first, of course, Vera could not believe her suspicions and even berated herself for having them. After about six weeks, she found herself facing up to the previously unthinkable thought that Neil might actually be thinking of leaving her. Outwardly calm, she was shocked, hurt and bewildered – utterly devastated. Naturally she looked to where she had gone wrong, what she had not done, etc. She found she had grown older.

She took to walking aimlessly. It was soothing, the more traffic the better, and spent hours and hours walking and thinking. She realized that this was a shocking blow to her pride: her trustingness had made her into a fool; she had never dreamed this sort of thing could happen to her family. It took time to work out a strategy, but she instinctively decided on a calm, serene front, with the appearance of being abstracted by the demands of the local hospital committee on which she sat. Neil saw her checking lists and so on.

Vera's greatest difficulty was in coming to terms with her pride. After all, she was a schoolteacher who could easily earn her own living. The realization that she might have to fight to keep her man turned into an awareness that she would have to fight *for* him. 'It was bad enough that *one* of us had lost all sense – I couldn't allow it to be both of us! It wasn't easy, it was probably the most difficult undertaking of my whole life, and looking back on it now I know I ought to be proud of it.' And yet she's not entirely proud. She still feels some residual humiliation, which is silly, she admits, especially when she reflects on what the state of herself and her family would have been now if she had not put up a fight.

> 'I would most probably have remarried or lived with someone – grovelled in gratitude to my new man for the smallest kindness he showed my kids – the sort of thing we expected from their own father – the kids would have had to spend some weekends with *her* and *her* delinquent twins – one has already been in trouble with the police for drugs. The lawyers would have had a field day over that. Neil

would have thought I was poisoning the children against him and, of course, *her*; he'd have believed that I was using her kids' teenage problems for my own vile ends. I know, because Neil and I have talked about it since then . . . now that it's all over . . . but I'll never get over her influence on him – the way she altered his thinking at that time. He actually told me that he thought a little bit of pot could be a very good thing. A health-freak like Neil! . . . *She* told Neil how unhappy she was with her own husband, said she never slept with him, the twins were only conceived because he raped her. And he believed her! At least he's not so naive, so gullible now.'

As for the ecstasy – where did that fit in and how had she handled it? Vera says now that she was lucky. She talked to a woman she hardly knew about it. The friendship and sympathy between the (strange) women who have shared this sort of desperation is immediate, and happens often enough to warrant mention. A Frenchwoman who was selling her a dress said how nice she looked in it, and Vera broke into tears, and told her everything. This woman told her not to be a fool, and suggested that if she must fight with Neil, it must be about anything but the Other Woman. Vera should buy a hi-fi or too many dresses – Neil and she could fight over extravagance, but if Neil should confess, she should admit that she knew but suggest that he should go away with the Other Woman to get it out of his system . . . which is exactly what happened: Neil went away, once the dimension of sin and secrecy was removed from his ecstasy, its pitch lowered accordingly.

In the end it was Vera who explained to Neil that this sort of thing happens to married men quite often, and if they are lucky they get over it without scattering ten lives to the winds. Nor could she resist adding that it's the mature married man who gets over it; the immature man does not, and has more regrets than anything else.

An understanding of the ecstasy/casualty connection has

endowed many a wife with the ability to wage a secret war. That such a war is not in every case a successful war goes without saying. Those who were defeated were able to draw some comfort and strength from their private awareness of having at least gone down fighting.

The strategy of secret defence means that a wife must first evaluate the seriousness of the threat. Some knowledge of the enemy is therefore essential, not only in terms of an assessment of the threat, but also in order to determine a strategy for defence. The case of Mavis indicates the tactical methods employed in an overall strategy of secret defence.

Mavis was first alerted to the possibility of the Other Woman when Ian stopped wearing a vest. They had been married for twenty-two years. Ian had a hairy chest which had always made him self-conscious. Indeed a medical report had once described him as being 'unusually hirsute'. Other than remarking that it was winter and that he could catch a bad chest cold – the temperature was below zero – Mavis said nothing.

Their children were away at university and although Ian had been a conscientious father he had never been enthusiastic about babies. His unexpected interest in a small baby at a supermarket, though fleeting, had earlier helped Mavis to conclude that the Other Woman must be a young mother with at least one small baby.

It was all too obvious that Ian had forgotten about babies that cried in the night. She decided that he ought to be reminded, and invented all sorts of stories about encounters with babies, and was often on the verge of recounting one of them but managed to stop herself in time. 'Some instinct made me stop myself. If he suspected I knew, I was sure I would be in even worse trouble.'

She had been making a routine search of Ian's pockets for about three weeks when she discovered a photograph of a lovely young woman with a child. She remembered thinking, 'Ah – the Madonna'. When her hands stopped shaking and she collected her thoughts, inspiration struck. She applied a magnifying glass to the photograph. A lengthy examination of the photograph revealed the existence of a wedding ring which explained why Ian's hours had not changed. The Other Woman was married, and not (as Mavis had suspected) divorced. The child, a girl, was, Mavis reckoned, between sixteen and twenty months. The handwriting on the back of the photograph read, 'Darling, Darling Ian. All my love, always. Yours forever, Jennie.' The handwriting appeared to Mavis to be 'immature and dull'. All of which meant, Mavis decided, that the danger was probably less acute than she had feared. Even so she was, she reports, shocked, hurt and terribly dismayed, but 'at 42 I wasn't about to be outwitted by a much younger woman!' She then took an important decision: to conceal everything she knew from Ian.

During the days and nights that followed, Mavis felt herself becoming listless and lethargic. 'My mind was racing around in circles, because I had no idea of what to do. I invented a back problem, so that my obvious distress could be put down to a tangible health difficulty.' It took about two weeks to hit on a strategy. She was aware of becoming more animated, but was careful to conceal this. 'I simply decided to borrow a baby. I would install the child in our home for a few days, and nights. . . .' But no baby library is yet in existence; it was not going to be as easy as all that, and time was of the essence. None of her friends had a small baby, and there was no baby-hire service. She began phoning various agencies offering her services – she would let a young overworked mother take a few days off. But no babies were available.

In the end she acquired her baby from an unlikely source. Her dentist's receptionist, a 25-year-old mother, was compelled to bring her baby to the surgery because there was no one to look after her. The baby was called Priscilla, and the young mother was called Carole.

Carole badly needed a rest, as she had had a difficult delivery, but who would take care of the baby? The dentist was in despair, for Carole was the best receptionist he had ever had. Mavis thought she just might be able to help.

Mavis was very careful about mentioning Carole's difficulties to Ian.

'I wanted to say it would prepare us for becoming grandparents, but I rather thought Ian would prefer to be a grandchild himself! I went about the preparation with a fury, and the day Priscilla arrived our house had been well and truly converted. It was almost like a hospital nursery. The house smelt of Dettol, and baby food, and that sweet smell of baby urine and baby crap. I made sure of all of that. These days you can get disposable nappies, but Ian didn't know that, and if he had asked I would have told him that Priscilla was allergic to man-made fibres.

'The house was cluttered up with baby equipment. A cot, a carry-cot, a stroller, a perambulator, a baby bath, a playpen, etc. Toys were scattered everywhere too. . . . The nappies had to be dried on the radiators. The smell was awful – really sour, curdled milk. . . . The place stank. . . .

'Priscilla was a delightful baby. So good: she slept through the night just as her mother said. So I reversed her sleeping hours. She slept through the day when Ian was at work, but the nights were terrible. It took just one night of waking the poor little thing. I still feel awful about that. Both Priscilla and I slept through the day. . . .

'Jennie's little girl was about eighteen months old. Of course Priscilla had to see her little cousin, Jake, who was 3½ years old. I invited Jake to spend a Sunday afternoon with Priscilla. Ian took his usual nap, but the noise disturbed him horribly.

'Ian said he couldn't understand how he could have forgotten the trials of small children. He couldn't wait for Priscilla's mother to come home.

'Priscilla was wonderfully co-operative – she threw up all over him twice, and wet his best trousers too. He looked ill and gaunt and haunted. He's a man who needs his sleep. Lots of sleep. He's needed lots of sleep for twenty-two years!

'About five weeks after Priscilla came to stay, Ian stopped exposing his chest. I still see Priscilla from time to time. Lovely child. She's my fairy godmother.

'Occasionally, Ian remarks on how much one can learn from a small baby. . . .

'Men of a certain age choose comfort, I think.'

Mavis waged a silent, secret, defensive war. Her counter-attack was invisible; perfect victory was dependent on the illusion that no war had been waged, that Mavis had remained blissfully ignorant that she had been both attacked and betrayed. Though the future is always invisible, her chief tactic was to make Ian's future with Jennie more tangible and, accordingly, more visible to him. . . . Her knowledge of the target, Ian, was superior to that of her adversary. She was better informed about his weaknesses, the most relevant of which was his active antipathy toward small, noisy children.

Two years later, Mavis inclines to the view that Ian had gone into the affair without thinking, and then let it continue without thinking. The little girl, Priscilla, probably alerted him to the consequences of what he might have been contemplating. Their relationship, she feels, has deepened and matured. She likes the idea that they each have a secret. Mavis would prefer never to tell him her secret, but if it became necessary; she thinks she might have to tell him. Her victory is unblemished because Ian emerged guilt-free, and Mavis therefore escaped the consequences of his guilty feelings towards her.

Ellen Barton was another of those wives who understood the ecstasy/casualty connection. She had known all about her husband Michael's affair for eight months but had consistently refused to indicate that she had the slightest suspicion, despite the usual clues: late nights, scented shirts, weekends away from home. But she wasn't going to make it easy for him, she decided; if he was so keen for her to know, he would tell her himself. She hoped he wouldn't say he wanted to go, and when, over dinner in their favourite Italian restaurant, that is precisely what he did say, she admitted having felt that something might have been wrong, but confessed to having tried not to allow suspicion and distrust to spoil things. Michael understood that, and was apologetic, even sad, but adamant. Biting her tongue, Ellen suggested that this sort of thing happened all the time, and wondered out loud (as she said) whether a trial period wouldn't be in his best interests, in everyone's best interests, really. It would be naive, of course, for anyone to expect a young girl, a very young girl, to comprehend anything like the 'sort of doubts that go hand in hand with maturity'.

She suggested a secret trial separation. Secret because she thought that it would be hard on Christine if she knew that it was only a trial period, so perhaps it would be kindest and wisest not to subject her to that sort of anxiety. (The truth was that she was certain Christine would not accept that and that the whole thing would become public which, of course, would make it harder when the time came for Michael to extricate himself.) His affair had been a secret for so long, a little longer wouldn't hurt. Meanwhile he and Christine could live together, more or less openly, though privately. It was a private affair, after all. . . . Besides, she would get used to being on her own and by the time – still to be arranged – that their friends got to hear about it, she would have had some time in which to recover. It was a way of preserving some dignity; in any case she'd rather go to pieces in private and without having to endure all that standard sympathy and shock. Their friends would find her serenely accepting, but for that, of course, she needed time. Besides, and this was by far the most important thing of all, they could remain real friends. She wasn't going to tell their son, Richard, there wasn't any real need – he was away at university and why upset him so soon?

Ellen took away far more than she gave. Michael lived

with Christine, but it was not quite clandestine enough, now. There was less excitement than he had thought. When it became necessary to lie to Christine about seeing Ellen, he decided that it was time to go home.

Lisa and her husband Aubrey, a decorator, have now been married for eight years. They have two children, aged 4 and 3. They were married when Lisa was 18 and Aubrey was 24. Lisa has always been besotted with Aubrey – she admits that most people can't understand why. Six years after they had been married, and soon after Aubrey's thirtieth birthday, Lisa got to know about Mary, who was the same age as Lisa, but whom Lisa knew only slightly.

Aubrey had become hostile; he flew into sudden rages with Lisa and with the small children. He had been a devoted and fond father; he now became irritable and impatient. One early evening, Lisa left the children with a neighbour, and asked Aubrey to go with her for a walk in the park. She told him that she knew about Mary. Aubrey said he loved her.

'I know you love her,' Lisa replied. 'But you don't love her more than me. You can't love her more than me.'

'I do,' Aubrey said. 'I love her more than I love you.'

'You don't mean it!' Lisa insisted.

'I mean it. I love her more.'

'But if we were both drowning, who would you save? Who?'

Aubrey answered, 'I'd push you down to save her.'

That night Aubrey left home. But Lisa promised him she'd wait for him. It didn't work out with Mary and, after six months, he came back.

Lisa's family and friends were outraged – 'don't have him back' they said. But she resisted all pressure. She was able to do this only because her family doctor told her to keep the door open, to let him know that he'd always be welcome, to take him back when the time came with open arms and without making any demands. There was no doubt, the doctor said, that Aubrey hadn't meant what he'd said. He was a lucky man because his wife was mature. Aubrey hadn't sowed his wild oats. Men were like that when they married young.

It had not been easy for Lisa to resist all that pressure from her friends and from her family.

> 'I knew in my heart that it was only sex that had made Aubrey say a thing like that. As soon as he said it, I knew. I wished he'd gone that mad with me, but I wasn't his girlfriend. Wives can't give their husbands that sort of madness. . . .'

Lisa was wise beyond her years. She told no one in her circle how Aubrey had answered her hypothetical question. The cruelty of his response was the measure of his madness.

An important ingredient of romantic love is the flight from reality. All that is real to ecstasy is itself. The husband who leaves home, wife and children to found a new nest for love instead of a nest for the young needs to be reminded of the other realities of his life. The Wallace story concerns a wife's dramatic and imaginative method of delivering just such a reminder to her husband.

The Wallaces had been married for seventeen years. They had four children and lived in the country. They kept a *pied-à-terre* in London. When Patrick and his new lover Anne (she was 24, Patrick 52) set up house together it was in that flat. Each Sunday Patrick came to visit his former family in the country and took the children out to lunch. Sarah endured this for four Sundays.

They were an orderly couple and had had their four children at regular intervals. Accordingly the children ranged in age from 11 to 2. Sarah took the following action. She hired a mini-cab and driver, loaded it with the four children and Bruce, a large and rather scruffy semi-Alsatian, and ordered the driver to take the children to the little lovenest in Chelsea. She armed the driver with Patrick's office number, just in case he was not there. She also packed a picnic hamper.

She asked the driver to deliver this note to Patrick:

Dear Patrick,

By the time you receive this I will be on my way to Los Angeles. Like you, I am following a thing that's bigger than me.

Clive needs extra attention to be given to his Latin. Laura has to have her anti-allergy shots every day this week. Simon, as you may or may not remember, is not yet old enough to go to school. Amanda is fairly capable, as you know, and has kindly offered to help Anne with the washing up. I'm told that Anne has given up work, so I know you won't be burdened with a babysitting problem, if only because you now have live-in help.

Simon may be allergic to dog hair and so to Bruce. But Dr Sanderson will let you know the test results as soon as he has them.

Much love,

Sarah

P.S. In case you have forgotten, they are on holiday.

Sarah called long distance from time to time. Amanda and Anne did not get along, and before too long it seemed Patrick and Anne did not get along too well, either. The siege lasted twenty-one days and then Anne surrendered unconditionally.

Sarah was as gentle in victory as he had been belligerent in war.

The intrusion of reality in the shape of four children and a dog was not the only reality to burst into Patrick's new lovenest. The other reality was in the shape of Anne who could not and would not tolerate those invaders from his other life.

Emerson's observation seems relevant here: 'Let us replace sentimentalism by realism, and dare to uncover those simple and terrible laws which, be they seen or unseen, pervade and govern.'

Certainly Sarah arranged to have sentimentalism replaced by realism. Her tactics were drastic but, as she says, necessary. From shattering the life of the family, the affair became one of those enriching episodes, a righted mistake of the kind that can even improve the past. All that happened nearly four years ago, and because the family was so nearly broken, it drew closer. Sarah's was a war of open sabotage, but she sent her legionnaires (her children) to do battle for her. Claire, the next example, opted for open confrontation in two phases. The first was to confront the Other Woman. Confrontation with her husband took place only after the Other Woman had briefed him to expect one. He was also briefed about the form the confrontation would take. He therefore had advance warning of the unorthodox nature of the proposals that would accompany the confrontation.

According to Claire, she and Mark had been married for twenty-eight pleasant years. They had three children, all of whom had left home. Apart from the usual traumas of adolescence, the children had presented few problems. Claire and Mark were devoted and conscientious parents, but had always pursued interests that were unrelated to their children. Their hobbies were collecting 'Sheffield' silver and golf. In other words, as Claire said, 'the bottom did not drop out of our world when the last of our children left the nest'. However, it was not long after this that Mark started to cancel golf games. Until then, nothing made Mark cancel, not the weather, not the state of his health and not the state of his business. 'Nothing short of a major catastrophe permits any sort of self-respecting golfer to cancel or, even worse, simply not turn up.'

> 'He started to become withdrawn and silent. . . . He had always been something of a sulk. He was ready to flare up over anything – the tuna casserole was not to his liking –

any event was an excuse to criticize me, not even when I got up the courage to ask him what was wrong.

'He had never been what you would call a flirt – he was almost old-fashioned – didn't mind telling or listening to the odd off-colour joke, but was otherwise rather square. He was the responsible sort who often said that he hoped he was a good Christian. And he meant this in the best possible way. In business he was known to honour his word – he had his own business and believed in fair play. He began muttering about business difficulties, about turning the whole thing up, about turning everything up. The last thing I thought of was another woman.

'I am not the jealous or suspicious type who searches pockets or reads other people's mail. But I found myself looking through Mark's pockets – I went through all his trousers, all his jackets, I even searched clothes he had not worn for years. In the end I found a phone number in someone else's handwriting in his winter coat. It was a very hot day – I remember well. It should have been easy, but it wasn't. I tried the usual thing like ringing that number to find out who the phone belonged to, but I never could find out – she answered the phone, but would not say who she was. I didn't want to be too obvious because I didn't want Mark to know that I was on to anything . . . in the end I went through the phone book; ruined my eyesight, I can tell you that. I simply read through every single number, started with A and had to wait until I got to L. Well, there it was, Martha Lowndes. So I drove over there and saw Mark's car. . . . She lived in a flat, so it didn't take long for me to know who she was or to find out what she did. And she was, of all things, a physiotherapist, 32 years old, and I have to say this – really plain. I mean ordinary – *really unattractive*. The funny thing is that I would not have been so alarmed if she had been better-looking. The way things were I knew she'd have to be trying very hard – this was an all-out effort on her part.

'Mark was about 52 at the time, and looked older, but an attractive man in the sense that he is tall, fairly muscular; you know, a very male-looking male. He couldn't eat and the weight just fell off him. It wasn't that he went on a diet – he could not eat. He looked tortured. The man was suffering, and I didn't look too good myself. In the end I talked to him. I thought about it, I thought long and hard before I told him that I'd had an anonymous phone call that had even named her name. I knew that Mark would never forgive me if he knew that I had gone through his pockets. . . . Mark seemed almost relieved. He said that Martha was like a drug, like cigarettes, he could not give her up. I didn't make a scene – don't ask me how I was so controlled, but I was, and thank God for that.

'During the next few days I didn't say much, didn't sleep much, didn't eat much. I even managed not to be hostile to Mark! All I did was think. . . . I increased my vitamin intake. I suppose you could say I was planning my campaign. After all, we'd had a good marriage and, besides, better the devil you know. . . .'

'I decided Martha and I should meet. So I called on her at work, during her lunch break. I visited the beauty shop first, took special care of what I wore and all that. You'd have thought I was going to meet a new lover! Martha was sweaty, you know what physiotherapists look like? She almost died when she saw me! But I was most polite. The first thing I told her was that I was glad Mark had got in tow with a decent *clean* sort of girl, and I managed to imply that all the scores of others had not been quite *so clean*, if you see what I mean? I told her that she could only be good for him – he was at that mid-life crisis. I was careful not to say he was menopausal in case she'd tell him – it might have obliged him to prove his extra virility. I made sure to tell her that Mark was a good and decent man, a family man who had also been a wonderful husband. She knew all that, she said. But she loved him too, and if I'd come to ask her to give him up, I was wasting my time.

'So I told her that I had come to see her because I had a constructive suggestion to make. She and Mark should go away together. Up until then Mark had not spent a whole night away from the family home. This way they could both see how they really got on. She would tell Mark that I had been to see her, and she should also tell him of my suggestion. Well, Martha told him, and they went away together.

'Of course, it was a gamble, but you see with one fell swoop I took away at least one vital ingredient from her magic potion, the taste of the clandestine, the forbidden. Well, after twenty-eight years you ought to know something about the man you've been living with, goddamn it! Mark was being a naughty boy in a big way, and as soon as I knew, the naughtiness lost some of that magic. The clandestine also meant a fair amount of guilt in Mark's case. I replaced or exchanged guilt for gratitude. He was so *grateful* to me. Grateful for my understanding, my sympathy, my sanity, my stability.

'That weekend made him see me in a new and better light. I injected a note of humour into the proceedings, too. Sent Martha flowers, sent them theatre tickets – to "The Constant Husband", wasn't I lucky! I lent her one of my dresses – a beautifully cut little black dress that displayed her massive masculine shoulders.

'Later, Mark told me the weekend hadn't been a real success . . . He'd kept thinking of me, wondered what I was doing, that sort of thing. He said he felt a heel, he knew he was behaving stupidly. . . . He kept remembering how I had asked him to promise not to feel guilty about me.

'I often wonder whether I was downright mean or downright smart. A bit of both – I think. Anyway, Martha was wrong for him. Mark would have been so *miserable*.'

Although Claire told her story with a fair degree of humour, it had been a profoundly disturbing experience. At 50, she is a sensible, humorous woman whose marriage means the world to her, the sort of woman who does not try to conceal her age, who allows the grey hairs in her short, shiny hair to show. Claire nevertheless wears her age with a youthful flair. She is pragmatic and, at the same time, imaginative. But her sporty, casual appearance is achieved by anything but a casual approach. She has an air of resilience rather than toughness.

But appearances, as they say, are deceptive. Four months after it was all over, Claire broke down. She couldn't eat, couldn't sleep, couldn't stop crying. She had what is known as a nervous breakdown, and was removed to a clinic for treatment. Her marriage to Mark was her second, and his first. Her first had been a youthful folly – a mistake that had no chance of being put right. That mistake, however, had produced one child, a daughter. Divorce proceedings had begun before the child was born. When Claire had met Mark, the child was two. Marriage to Mark had meant leaving her country, which had meant leaving her small daughter with her former husband.

Small wonder then, that Claire reacted to Mark's betrayal of all that had gone before with a disabling depression. Mark found it intolerably difficult to discuss the problem with the psychiatrist-in-charge, and rushed weeping from his office. He was certain that he wanted the marriage to continue. Claire recovered. Now, five years later the marriage continues, though Claire feels that 'it is not the same; in some ways it is better'.

The costs of victory are high. But the costs of defeat would probably have been higher still. Mark and Claire are kind with one another, and careful, but Claire knows and can't stop herself from being 'difficult sometimes, usually for no reason at all'. Mark's family life is important to him, and Claire believes that he's relieved at the way things turned out, and possibly even grateful to her. She loves him, but no longer trusts him. She wonders whether love without trust is love.

Lucy fought a variation of the secret war. It was a subtle war fought on two fronts, for Lucy waged war with her husband as well as with the Other Woman. Lucy is a housewife as well as an art historian but when the war was fought, fifteen years ago, she was a full-time housewife.

> 'Fred suddenly began keeping later and later hours. He was an engineer, and was deeply involved in his company's expansion programme. I understood this, we discussed his work and he often sought my advice on his colleagues. He liked to have my opinion on that sort of thing. Anyway it was quite a while before I began to think there might be some sort of sinister reason for his late arrivals home. We'd been married for fifteen years, I was 38 years old at the time, and I remember reading a novel one night with less than my usual concentration. At around midnight I suddenly looked at my watch, and thought, It's late, very late. In fact it's bloody late.
>
> 'And then I felt angry with him. I was mad, furious, but, fortunately, as it turned out, I was very, very tired. Exhausted. So I fell asleep. Which, in the event, saved everything. Because if I had not been asleep we would have had the most unholy row. I would have behaved like a shrew, and screamed out all my half-baked suspicions. And I know I would have thrown him out. I would have had to have saved face. I was that sort of person for one thing, and for another we both prided ourselves on not having a modern marriage. Indeed, we used to say – we were somewhat pretentious in those days – we haven't got a modern marriage, we've got a good one instead. So you can understand what I mean when I say I was lucky enough to fall asleep.
>
> 'The next morning I awoke earlier than usual, and I remember watching Fred as he lay peacefully asleep. I studied him, and suddenly faced the thought that I could

be left – that Fred could leave me. That possibility had never occurred to me before. Now, though I saw the possibility as remote, it was nevertheless a possibility, and that was bad enough in itself. I remember sitting up and actually saying out loud, "Now, Lucy my girl, put your thinking cap on." I was very calm, I remember that.

'Things began to fall into place. His secretary, Jean, had become more and more important. Fred called her his right hand. She was fairly attractive, not much younger than I, but you could tell she'd never had children. She was devoted to Fred, and an excellent secretary. Fred had to visit building sites, and Jean used to drive him around quite a bit. She often brought him home, and I used to invite her in for a drink. We were on first name terms, she called me Lucy, and was generally very helpful. But that morning, as I studied Fred asleep, I remembered having seen her once run her fingers through his hair. I was upstairs, she had brought him home, and I happened to glance out of the window and saw them sitting in the company car. I realized that I had put it out of my mind at once. Even now I was not sure why. But I really did put it out of my mind. Shut it out. But recalling it so unexpectedly was like seeing it happen for the first time, except that it was as if I was examining what I was seeing, like a doctor.

'And then the extra razor blades made sense. Fred is quite frugal with his personal requirements, but had suddenly begun to require more and more razor blades. He was busy and highly preoccupied with the firm's expansion, as I said earlier, and our sex life had gone in for a quiet spell. And I, in recognition of his manifold duties and responsibilities and with, I freely admit, an eye to his career opportunities, had become less and less demanding in all areas.

'I resolved to change all this. The whole plan, or, as you would say, strategy, unfolded before me in less than five minutes. It may have been that I was thinking, subconsciously, along these lines for some time, but I can truthfully say that I had not been alert to any real danger. I knew that I could not get rid of her via direct means, the only action open to me was indirect action. A great departure from my norm, I want you to know. . . .

'I first directed my attention to Fred, and how to handle him. I decided to make more demands on him, not only as far as our own four children were concerned, but I'd let him handle a little bit more of the burden of his parents for himself. They were rather elderly. I used to collect them on Sundays and have them spend the day with me while he went off on his site inspections. This became increasingly difficult for me to arrange, and Fred was obliged to help out. They were his parents after all. He's the gregarious sort, and liked to go to, and to give, dinner parties. But in deference to his busy life I'd sidestepped a lot of these gatherings because I'd believed he was so tired. I was genuinely concerned for his health. But it was true that he was tired, just as it was true that he was a very valuable senior executive. I began to campaign for him to have a driver, spoke to his colleagues and so on at the innumerable dinner parties I found myself giving, and Fred very soon had his own driver. He really did need one – I ought to have seen to that before. However, there was no longer any need for Jean to drive him anywhere.

'I also became far more aggressive and, frankly, more demanding, on the sexual front. In short, I took the initiative, and I want to tell you that in the process I found I had more talent in that area than I had ever even hoped for. That helped.

'Fred called Jean his right hand. I took to calling her my left hand. I loaded her up with all sorts of tasks, would ask her to book theatre tickets, would ask her to send flowers to business associates, would ask her to call the travel agent for our family holiday – things like that. "I hate to have to ask my left hand again!" I would say, "but Fred wants to invite the Hugheses to the first night of such and such, and if they had to dine with us first wouldn't my left hand like to check which dates would be suitable to the Hugheses?"

'Doing all these things for me must have killed her. Two months after that decision of mine she found another job, and I was properly sympathetic about the loss of such an efficient secretary. Fred and I have never discussed her, in any other role. About six weeks after she had left, I received something in the mail. It was a photocopy of a letter Fred had written to Jean six months earlier when she was at her most powerful, and he at his most vulnerable. It was a passionate letter, frankly erotic. He was searching for a way, he said to resolve his family problems so that Jean and he could be together. . . . So you see he *had* actually thought of leaving. . . . But I will go to my death denying ever having received such a letter. . . . If I were asked, that is, which I somehow doubt.'

Like Lucy, several wives were offered proof, after the event, that an affair had taken place. In some cases irrefutable evidence was presented to a wholly unsuspecting wife. If Jean had hoped to bring matters to the boil, to resuscitate a dead affair, Lucy successfully neutralized her attempt. Lucy's chief concern was to avoid giving the episode any sort of importance whatsoever. The affair, though, had been of overwhelming importance to Lucy, but that was a very private matter. For her part, Lucy proved that assumed ignorance can be as blissful as the real thing. Her assumed ignorance has freed her from having to endure the complication of her husband's feelings of guilt. No one likes being made to feel guilty, and their mutual discretion (or deception) saved both from the ramifications of guilt.

Even for a graduate of Harvard Business School, Wayne's career was extraordinarily successful. At 32 he was one of the vice-presidents of a multinational steel corporation. His wife, Drew, who had been a fashion co-ordinator, had changed jobs when their baby, Sam, was born. She had exchanged one form of full-time employment for another –

mothering. Sam was five months old when she overheard Wayne confirming his arrangements with Stella. He was to leave the next day. It was the tone of his voice that made her stop in her tracks and listen with acute attentiveness. His voice was a low, husky, sexy drawl; she had known it well – it was why she had married him. He used it as some men use cigarette lighters – on special occasions only.

Drew checked his booking with the airline, and then decided on a dangerous plan of action. He would usually put his suitcase on the back seat, drive himself the two-hour journey to the airport and park his car there, so as to drive himself home. He usually packed his luggage about half-an-hour before he left – that way he could attend to his last-minute needs in peace. Drew decided that he could do with some extra luggage – she loaded Sam in his carry-cot into the back of the car. She prayed the baby would not wake for at least an hour, so that when he turned round again she could be well on her way to a nearby motel. She left a note on the kitchen table saying that she knew of his plans, but had decided she was more in need of a holiday than he. She'd said she'd call to check on how things were going, but her destination was private. She did not tell him that she would keep calling until she got a reply, and if there was no reply, she would go to the airport to retrieve her baby.

The baby woke after three-quarters of an hour, and Wayne could not believe his ears, he thought he was hearing things. He stopped the car to investigate and when he discovered his own baby son he thought he was seeing things. He did what his wife had predicted he would do – he turned around and sped home.

Drew called twice a day for five days and then she returned home. She told Wayne that she thought it would do him good to get on intimate terms with his own son. As Drew says, now, 'I left *him* holding the baby!' Wayne was shocked, but bemused by his wife's tactics; her behaviour was awesome, and he found himself awed by her daring, by her bravery. Never, not in a million years, could he have predicted that his wife could have been capable of such behaviour; he thought he would really like to get to know such a woman. There couldn't be another one like her, he was certain; not one, not in all creation. He was married to a marvel, a marvel who, to do such a thing, must have thought a hell of a lot of *him*.

Their reunion was an ecstatic mixture of humour, tenderness, shock and warning. Wayne and his baby son had indeed become better acquainted. A day or two after their reunion Wayne told Drew that he wanted more children, but Drew said no, not for ten years. Until then, he would be on trial. She said this with the grimmest determination; she was uncompromising: *no more second chances*. Their second son was born when Sam was 11 years old.

Drew's strategy was more than somewhat extreme. Her anxiety over the untended baby in the back seat of Wayne's car haunts her still, as ten years later she considers what might have been. What if Wayne had been compelled to brake suddenly? He knew nothing of the priceless contents in the back of his car. . . . She believes that her actions were dictated by her ice-cold fury – Wayne was not going to be allowed to get away with leaving the wife to hold the baby.

Drew's reaction may have been hysteria of a certain kind. It did not, however, take a conventional shape. That none of the women mentioned here lapsed into a classical form of hysteria does not mean that the knowledge of the Other Woman did not hurt. All of them had a profound understanding of male sexuality. They also understood, however primal their understanding, that men are far more prone than women to abandoning a family on purely sexual grounds. Few women as yet have the flexibility to be taken over and overwhelmed by their sexual senses with anything quite like the facility that has been given to men. Therefore those who will undoubtedly claim that any reference to the differences between male and female sexuality is 'sexist' will not be wrong. It is sexist in the sense that the male aptitude for promiscuity is greater than the female aptitude for promiscuity. Those men who have contributed to a sperm bank take pleasure even in the thought of having sired progeny, those women who have given their babies up for adoption take no pleasure from that knowledge. On the contrary, depression is a common consequence.

One of the by-products of the contraceptive revolution is that, though sex is as readily available as Coca-Cola, the double standard still stands. Because women's reproductive organs are protected from unwanted reproduction, their need to protect their existing families from outside predators has become no less, and perhaps more, vital than it ever was. Freedom always implies responsibility and a price. Although free in their bodies from unwanted consequences such as pregnancy, a terrible price has been extracted. For it has become necessary for women to protect their families from dangerous female human predators.

However various were the tactics deployed, the same goal, that is the preservation of the family, was common to all the women referred to here. It is likely that this primal understanding of the male aptitude for promiscuity owes more than a little to an intellectual awareness of natural injustice.

4

Seductive mothering: the strategy of diplomacy

If we accept the illusory qualities of romantic love, we must also accept that it is an imitation of unconditional love, like mother love. For in all mothering there is a certain healthy sensuality. Part of the magic of romantic love is the way failings and weaknesses and even irritations are transformed into charm, grace or brilliance. Some wives' counter-offensives to the Other Woman are to give this sort of apparently unconditional love, or if not, then an adequate semblance of it. Some husbands go as far as asking their wives not to make it easy for them to leave. They may do this indirectly, 'I love you, but I'm in love with her – I know she'll never be as good for me as you have been – but I can't help myself, I'm crazy about her.' Others say, 'Love me more if you can.' More in this case means more than she does, more than you do – more and more and still more, and more, still, than all.

Some men have a need to reveal, however obliquely, their own burdens and, though inadmissible, because it is held to be unmasculine, their fragility. Now most wives will tell you that they want to be wives and not mothers; some wives, however, will admit that the two are not necessarily mutually exclusive. But the mothering has been systematically downgraded; women want to be more than mothers, and rightly so, but too often deprive themselves of expressing that which is uniquely and instinctively theirs – the art and the skill, indeed the gift of mothering. For all cant to the contrary, the expression of motherly sentiment is one of the most fundamentally rewarding of all the expressions of womankind but, sadly, it is a gift, a reward that is being lost, negated and outmoded. Mothering stands in the way of progress, it impedes independence – and personal growth, it seems, can only be achieved independently.

It is perhaps significant that the efficacy of mothering is evident in these cases where a husband leaves for the Other Woman who is considerably older than his wife, and sometimes even older than him. At any rate, generous, though essentially subtle applications of poultices of loving, tender care, appear to go a long way towards lowering the fever pitch of spiralling ecstasy.

Ellis, 33, a public relations executive, could not get rid of Sheila, 22. It had gone on for about a year, and his wife, Betty, 35, knew nothing about it. They'd been married for ten years. He decided to confess everything to Betty, to ask for her help. He wanted Betty to tell Sheila that she knew about her, knew how she wouldn't leave Ellis alone. Betty did just this, and afterwards said that she 'felt like a mother getting her kid out of trouble. Making excuses and so on.'

Elaine and Richard met when they were the same age, 22, while Richard was still a medical student, in his second year of study. Richard's mother, widowed and disabled, was 58, and in need of financial as well as physical assistance. Because Richard was an only child, it seemed right for his mother to live with them. Elaine, a highly efficient executive secretary to the chairman of an international insurance company, took on extra work and typed at home. She supported them all, and was not resentful. She was fairly plump, dressed neatly and was, as she says, an 'ordinary-looking girl'. Though tall, Richard was otherwise pretty ordinary-looking himself. Photographs of that time show an earnest, serious Richard, whose black-rimmed glasses made his long and broad nose longer, his narrow forehead narrower. When he graduated it was hard to tell who was the more proud, his mother or Elaine.

But the hard years of study and exams were not yet over. It had long been decided that Richard would specialize in gynaecology and obstetrics. Their first child was born after Richard qualified as a doctor – he'd had to repeat a year – but before he became a specialist. Elaine typed at home. It was found that she had become infertile and so her son, like his father, was an only child. Richard's brilliant exam results made him a consultant at 35, and soon he had a private practice. He became a fashionable doctor whose patients adored him. His looks turned from ordinary to distinguished. He was prematurely grey and the hair that was once greasy was now worn in a stylish youthful cut. The hairdresser was the husband of a grateful patient.

Everyone agreed that, on the face of things, Melissa, 22, trendy, long, wild blonde hair, with a prestigious job in the publicity department of a publishing company, was better suited to Richard than Elaine had been. Elaine, after all, was rather plump, rather dowdy; all those years of typing, of caring for Richard's mother, for Richard's son, for Richard, *showed*. Besides, she hadn't really grown, hadn't kept up with him, after all, he had his image to think of. Who could blame him?

The awful thing is that Elaine agreed with everyone, including her mother-in-law. Her friends told her they wouldn't put up with that sort of thing – she should divorce. Her outraged parents, her sister, and even her brother, advised her to get out, to stop humiliating herself by begging him to give Melissa up. She had asked them to speak to Richard – 'someone should speak *for* me,' she'd pleaded – but they'd refused. Get rid of him! Tell the bastard to go to hell! Take him to the cleaners! Perhaps she had always been forced to be more of a mother than a wife. But she and Richard were still friends, and though rare, their lovemaking was not non-existent – the man-wife connection was still alive. She was persuaded to deliver an ultimatum: Richard chose Melissa. They lived together for fourteen months and then Melissa left.

Richard went back to Elaine. He has a new girlfriend now. Elaine has learned to believe in safety in numbers; she has learned to hope for others, for, as she sees it, she still has her husband, she is not the doctor's divorced wife, but his wife. They are invited to dinner parties and to gala banquets, and Elaine enjoys these. She is convinced that life with a faithless husband is better than a life with no husband. 'The family is together again – all of us – even Richard; we are much, much happier than we were during those fourteen terrible months.'

The Other Woman usually comes to terms with the fact that her married man – who still lives with his wife – goes to bed with his wife as well. For many this is an acceptable infidelity, but she tends to be faithful to him. Some wives turn away from their husbands while the crisis is on, because they find they cannot endure his coming to their bed directly from the bed of another. Others find his infatuation curiously aphrodisiacal and confound both the Other Woman and their husbands with the sheer inventiveness of their energy, and some spouses make love as a form of comforting one another, much in the way they would hold and comfort a distressed child, for in comforting another, you often comfort yourself.

'Jock was so miserable, moving between the two of us,' said Karen, 33, married for fourteen years.

> 'We were talking about it one night, and he didn't know what to do. Couldn't decide what he really wanted. He broke down, and sobbed. He's not like that. I got in the chair with him, and almost put him on my lap. He was half on my lap. I put his head against my breast, like you do with one of the kids . . . cuddled him. Then it turned to

lovemaking. It's hard to explain, but I think for both of us it was more comforting than sexual.'

But this is a form of comfort that some husbands cannot bring themselves to provide, either from the literally immobilizing effect of guilt, or because they cannot be unfaithful to the Other Woman. Still others use up all their sexual strength, and there is not enough to go round, though this happens less frequently than one would imagine.

Little is as painful to a wife as the knowledge that her husband no longer desires her. Some wives, humiliated and hurt, are too embarrassed, or too angry, or too fearful of failure to even begin to think of trying to seduce their own husbands. But some do.

Dawn, 48, and a geography teacher, was one of those wives who successfully seduced her husband and abandoned the role of mother. Tim was a catering manager at a private hospital. Their fifteen-year marriage had been successful, they had two daughters aged 14 and 12, and, according to Dawn, their family life was amiable. But then Tim became involved with his secretary Valerie who at 31 had been divorced for five years. Dawn believed the affair had been going on for about five months before she had any clues. She realized something was going on when Tim began answering the telephone – he usually left that to someone else because he hated the phone. One night, shoeless, she crept downstairs and overheard him talking to Valerie. By this time their sex life had dwindled and, in common with so many other wives, Dawn put this down to pressures and difficulties at work. Tim had told her the hospital were retrenching, he had been compelled to make three people redundant, and this had depressed him.

Tim had no sooner replaced the receiver than Dawn demanded to speak to him – *privately* – in their bedroom. The girls were still awake, but Dawn didn't even try to stop herself from forcing an immediate confrontation, something she says she will always regret. First, she told him she knew he was having an affair, to which he replied that that was quite true, and then she said that if he was planning on leaving her and the girls he ought to tell her at once. He was thinking about it, he said, he didn't know what he wanted to do, yet, except that he would not give up Valerie. It was then that Dawn felt her mind go numb, yet she began to shiver, as if she had caught a severe chill. Her very teeth chattered, and Tim who had seen this happen to her before when she really had caught a chill, offered to make her a cup of tea. It was while he was in the kitchen that Dawn's mind went into emergency gear. She realized that she had expected Tim to deny everything. Everything fell into place – those two occasions when he had failed to achieve orgasm owed nothing to those redundancies he had spoken of. She questioned, fleetingly, whether there had in fact been any redundancies in the first place. When he brought her the hot tea he held it to her lips and fed her, and after forcing it down Dawn told him that she would wait for him to get the whole thing out of his system. She said she wanted to blank the whole thing out, just for tonight. She asked for sleeping pills. She said she felt sick, really sick.

Though Tim slept beside her throughout that long sleepless night, Dawn's incessant awareness that it was she who had brought it out into the open meant, she knew, that there would be no turning back. She did not go to work but stayed in bed all that day and all the next. On the third day, Tim phoned to say he would not be coming home that night, but he would be in for dinner the following night. So it was on the third day that Dawn reached the fullest, coldest and, as she emphasizes, most *honest* understanding of the danger she and her daughters faced. A strategy began to unfold; somehow she would get that man back into bed with her. She could not as yet imagine quite how this could be done, she knew only that it must be done. On the fourth day she telephoned his office and left a message with the switchboard, and *not* with Tim's secretary, Valerie, reminding him not to be late; she was going to serve a roast. She hated Valerie, but hated her purely and roundly too. She swore to herself that Valerie would be made redundant in every way.

On the fourth day, again, Dawn did not turn up at school. She found herself thinking rationally, calmly; she even began to warm to the battle. She reviewed her marriage, she reviewed Tim's marriage and decided that while her marriage had become comfortably dull, his marriage had become comfortably boring. Somewhere in his mind, Tim had to know that it had been a good marriage. But then he had lost his mind.

That was the last day that Dawn was to play truant, but she used the day well. She examined her body, stretched with tension – it ached. Her face was haggard, scaled with fear; her eyes hurt and lifeless. Her face, swollen but gaunt, appeared to have aged ten years. But she had been fairly attractive once – four days ago.

The plan that had been forming consolidated. She was grimly aware of the multitudes of wives who had made the same plans before her. Some of them must have succeeded. Even more important, though, the girls must make no mention of the change in her appearance in front of their father. (It would also be a lesson, for them, in guile.)

Massaging brings comfort, brings relief; Dawn's mind, soothed, received an idea. She would learn massage, would learn to soothe. The masseuse was helpful, and told her where to go. Dawn confided her problem. The masseuse suggested yoga; it helps people, she said. The beginnings of hope glimmered along with a new plan.

When Tim came home that night Dawn saw that he was apprehensive, suspicious and even hostile. When the girls were asleep she told him what she had planned to tell him. She loved him, and would wait for him. He would want to spend more time with Valerie and she understood that; but she hoped he wouldn't leave home. She'd made excuses to the girls about the nights he didn't come home.

Dawn endured Valerie for four tense months. The seduction, when it was attempted, would have to be subtle. No outrageous lingerie, nothing to frighten him. He would have to be taken, quite literally, unawares. He would have to want her the way a man can want any *anonymous* woman. . . . But timing, or rather the choice of timing, would be crucial.

The books she read, from pornography to clinical sex manuals, fuelled her fantasies of making love to him, of teaching him what sex was all about, of fucking him to kingdom come, of showing him what a hell of a woman he was married to. She was as shameless in her thinking as she was in her actions – masturbation, she decided, was bad for the soul, but good for the body. Those magazine articles had been right. She toyed with the idea of flirting with her male colleagues, of picking up a man, any man. She dreamed of driving Tim wild, and then throwing him out. Meanwhile she was becoming an expert in yoga.

During the fourth month Dawn decided it was do or die. One night she left Tim watching a tennis match, went upstairs and began her yoga. Tim had never before seen her in a leotard, and when she heard him mounting the stairs, she stood on her head and arranged her legs in the provocative way that she had been practising for so long.

It worked.

For Dawn it was four months but, astonishingly, some wives endure the ongoing threat of the Other Woman for forty years, never quite sure whether or not he will stay. Theirs is the man who has decided on having two (or more) women permanently in his life. But the husband who is in a *crisis of indecision* is the one whose decision is largely linked to his wife's handling of the Woman versus Woman conflict. And once the affair is out in the open, and the dimension of secrecy that did so much to heighten its elements has been lost, it is the wife's attitude that is, in the end, a fairly decisive factor. Recalling this period in their lives, many wives referred to having slipped into emergency gear, or turned to some form of crisis management, or put on the brakes, or told themselves to keep calm, to stop and think, or to take it easy. Those who managed to deflect their husbands from leaving, however temporarily, went in for a holding operation, and hoped to buy time. It is not altogether surprising that most of those wives who negotiated successfully suggested that their husbands consider what they would be doing to themselves, and refrained from any mention of what his desertion would do to his family, or to his wife. Interestingly enough, this feat (for feat it is) was even managed by young women in their twenties. It is perhaps a rather sad reflection on the male state since it reflects an essential male selfishness. On the other hand, those wives realized that the Other Woman had happened because the husband had suddenly found himself trapped by the marital state, and longed to cut loose from it, rather than to be caught again, though in a newer trap. For it would appear that most women have given some form of conscious or subconscious thought to what they would do if ever they were compelled to face the threat of the Other Woman. Many react entirely differently from the way they had anticipated, especially those who had been certain that they would opt for immediate divorce. Curiously, it is often these very women who switch from avenger to negotiator, sometimes with dazzling brilliance, and sometimes with the aim of inflicting a similar condition on their husbands later, in their own good time. It is safe to say that a man considering leaving his wife and children is far more involved with his own and possibly his Other Woman's welfare and wellbeing than with the fate of those he plans to leave behind. It is for this reason that pleas such as 'how can you do this to me/to us?' not only fall on deaf ears but are counterproductive as well.

The following brief excerpts from case histories illustrate certain negotiation techniques, as well as the thinking that lay behind the handling of the husband's condition, to say nothing of the launching of an undercover blast in the Woman versus Woman conflict.

Hilary, a fashion buyer aged 28, knew that her husband, Gilbert, 32, was ruled by his ambition. Both his parents had always worked in factories, his mother in a food-freezing plant and his father in motor assembly. Gilbert was proud of being a lawyer. He was a junior partner in a particularly crusty and puritanical legal partnership. He was definite about leaving her to go to his secretary, Jess. Hilary did not ask him to stay. Instead she suggested that he sort through his things – it would take about two nights, and she could make good use of the space he would have cleared. He agreed, Hilary believes, most probably because her lack of hysteria was a terrible shock to him. It was while he was going through his things that Hilary wondered out loud quite how his partner would take this. Would Mr Thurston, the senior partner, accept Jess? Had Gilbert given enough thought to whether or not Jess would fit in? She mentioned those interminable country weekends at the Thurstons. She giggled, as she remembered aloud, about the coveted invitations to those weekends. She supposed that Gilbert wouldn't have to put up with that sort of thing any more. She really hoped this wouldn't damage his career too much. . . .

That Hilary managed not to sound sarcastic owed everything to will, and nothing to her real feelings. This is another example of diminishing the Other Woman without at the same time diminishing the man. Hilary never said this aloud, but the clear implication was that Jess didn't really come up to *his* high standards. This sort of talk, about *his* professional aspirations, *his* life-style, about what was best for *him*, was their usual sort of talk. It was also a way of indicating that though what was happening to Gilbert was unusual and earth-shattering, it was also part of the usual scheme of things, it happened often, it happened to most men. Gilbert didn't have to leave home, he could continue with his affair. But Jess couldn't live like that any more, he had been adamant; she had told him that he would simply have to choose.

Hilary countered that by saying that though she couldn't really blame Jess for that ultimatum, it wasn't fair to put a man under that sort of pressure. She herself could never do a thing like that. It looked as if Jess would always *expect* to come first, before his career, before everything. She wondered how he would cope with being one of those slavish sorts of husbands. It already looked as if he was a bit frightened of Jess. He wasn't frightened of her, only of losing her, he countered. Hilary supposed he would learn to live with that. He'd probably always be frightened of that. It seemed likely that she was the sort of person who was used to getting her own way, no matter at what cost. That wasn't a bad thing, but what about the cost to *him*?

The final example in this category is that of Emma, 38, second wife of Frank, 59, a personnel director. Frank and Emma had one child, a daughter aged 5. Now Frank wanted another divorce, this time for Ivy, 28, who resembled Emma, as Emma resembled Marilyn, his first wife. Emma said nothing about this. She concentrated, instead, on how Marilyn would gloat about his newest venture. She also wondered how Ivy would manage on only a quarter of what she had had, considering how much alimony he had already paid out to Marilyn. She also hoped that Ivy would get a better deal from Marilyn's children than she had had. She thought it would be fun for him to watch his newest brood playing alongside his grandchildren. It was too bad that there wasn't really enough money to go round as it was; Ivy probably wouldn't mind a bedsit, but what about Frank – would he get used to that? If it hurt her even to think of Frank's living like that, what it would do to him didn't bear thinking about. He'd worked so hard, too, all his life. . . . Still, Ivy probably thought life in a bedsit would be romantic. She was young enough to believe that.

These examples are all concerned with negotiation. Hilary and Emma concentrated their negotiation on a consideration of what would be in their husband's best interests. What would be best for *him*? How would the change affect *his* work, *his* finances, *his* standard of living, *his* boys? At the same time each wife showed herself to be loving, considerate, undemanding, unhysterical and rational. The Other Woman had applied the pressure; there was no need for them to as well. After all, their husband was what he had always been: his wife's first interest, first consideration, first priority. Not one of the men questioned why his wife was putting him and his wellbeing ahead of hers. To ask what is good for *me* is a very different thing from asking what is good for the family. . . .

Anne knew it was happening all over again when Keith, who never read novels, began reading Graham Greene. The last time, four years ago, he'd developed a passion for German expressionist art; Druscilla had been a History of Art student. She wondered what sort of girl had sent him to Graham Greene. She also wondered how many more times she would have to go through this sort of thing. She was 36, attractive, dressed conventionally to suit her executive role as director of a company that made knitting machines. She owned one of these herself, used it expertly, and was an excellent walking advertisement for the product.

They'd been married for fourteen years, and had the standard two children, two dogs, two cars. It was a pleasant enough life. Keith had a workshop in which he made all sorts of useful bookshelves. At least the Graham Greenes would find a home – when the right time came they'd go in the bookshelves in the basement, where they belonged.

She wished Keith would conduct his love affairs the way women conducted theirs. She, too, had developed new and passionate tastes and interests. She'd even read the sports pages, but never in front of Keith, of course. They loved each other enough to be mutually supportive. He appreciated her dress and cooking, and said so. She appreciated his work and his bookshelves, and said so. Of course, she'd risked her marriage, and more than once, but because she had no doubts that the marriage would end as soon as Keith knew, she did her best to minimize the risk. The one thing she did not risk was the loss of control – no affair of hers would ever dare become bigger than her family. From her point of view, all her affairs were harmless.

Her strategy had worked four years ago. Then she'd been understanding about his irregular hours, irregular absences, his irregular lovemaking. After about six weeks of that, Anne put her husband to bed. He'd come home one night, late, at about 3 a.m. Anne pretended he'd awakened her and sleepily switched on the bedside lamp, said a dreamy 'hello', then sat up and said sharply, 'What's the matter – you look *ill*!' She didn't wait for a reply but got up hurriedly, wondering aloud where the hell the thermometer had got to; he looked so flushed. She found it in the bathroom – she knew all along where it was because she'd doctored it by putting it under the tap – and while he was still undressing, pushed it in his mouth. His temperature was where she'd set it – 2 degrees above normal.

Anne believes that 'to do this sort of thing, you have to know your husband very very well.' Like many women her theories on men are based on one man – her husband. According to Anne,

> 'Most men are cowards, and terrified of illness. A cold is enough to send Keith to despair. He groans and sniffs and sighs and clears his throat. He hardly ever gets a real cough, but coughs all the same. They're all schoolboys at heart. I make him jelly and lots and lots of hot toddies and triple measures of whisky, juice of a full lemon, a little water and a tablespoon of honey. Having a cold is a nuisance, but it's also a treat. It was just as well I'd fixed the thermometer. Keith asked to see it that night.'

She kept him in bed for two days and fed him jelly and hot toddies and changed his pyjamas and changed his sheets, soothed his brow, offered to read to him, but he felt too ill, he said, and couldn't concentrate. On the morning of the third day he felt well enough to go to work, and fit enough to make love again. By artificially raising his temperature, she lowered the heat of his passion.

In some instances *both* the husband and the wife are frightened of the Other Woman, afraid, as of an elemental force. Both acknowledge her power, and both feel powerless to resist. It is as if the Other Woman, and the grip of her passion, is in some inexplicable yet certain way the expression and the representative of their combined destiny, their mutual fate. Maureen and Syd had been married for two years. They had lived together for ten years before taking the marital vows that were so important to them. They both believed that they 'didn't really deserve so much happiness', none of their friends had anything like their 'significant and deep relationship'. A year after their marriage, however, Syd's personality began to change. Maureen was convinced they were 'still very deeply in love'. Syd grew quieter, became critical, was hard to please. When they went away on holiday for three weeks he made love to her only three times. Holidays usually meant sex every night.

Maureen, like many a wife, like many a woman in love, had sometimes teased herself with the hypothetical question of what she would do if ever she found out that Syd was unfaithful to her. (It is noteworthy how many wives admit to asking themselves this question no matter at what level of their consciousness.) Maureen decided that she could tolerate a one-night stand, if she had to, but no more than that.

They were a serious, responsible couple; Maureen taught retarded children and Syd, a successful financial analyst, was also the captain of his tennis club. They were obliged to entertain at home, and Maureen was good at this. When she found out about the Other Woman (also called Maureen) she and Syd had already decided to have a baby.

Maureen staunchly maintains that she had neither been searching nor conducting an investigation when she discovered the other Maureen's letters. She had been clearing out a cupboard when a shoe box fell down and scattered the contents, amongst which was a photograph of a nude, flat-chested woman and an envelope marked 'Maureen's letters'. She studied the photograph thinking at first that Syd had brought it home after one of his stag nights. He usually showed her the pictures of the girls who had been on show. But Syd was a 'bosom man', and this bosomless girl, therefore, aroused Maureen's curiosity. The handwriting on the envelope was unfamiliar to her, but she opened the envelope because, strangely, that handwriting might very well have been her own. Occasionally Maureen had sent Syd love letters and disguised the handwriting on the envelope, it was a little ruse that had surprised and delighted him. But these sexually explicit love letters had been written by another woman. Like so many wives in her position, Maureen resolved to say nothing to her husband, and again like so many wives similarly placed, burst into tears as soon as he walked through the front door. Although Syd was deeply distressed by what he called Maureen's 'suffering', he said he was glad she knew – he couldn't stand the deceit any longer. (Curiously, several wives reported that their husbands found something rewarding in the knowledge that the Other Woman meant that their wives suffered *for* them.)

It was decided that he would continue seeing the other Maureen, and this he did, three or four times a week, for about four months. Meanwhile, the other Maureen had also noticed a 'personality change' in Syd, begun, she said, as soon as his wife found out. Syd wanted to break it off, wanted to get rid of her, but couldn't. The other Maureen marched into his office and told him that she would refuse to let him go. His life was crumbling about him, and he was in a 'terrible state, near collapse but he just could not get rid of the woman.' Her sexual grip over him was strangling him: he knew this, but could not escape. His wife couldn't stand the strain and left him for two weeks, but returned towards Christmas, for 'family reasons'. They didn't want their relations to know. Not yet, anyway. . . .

Syd did not know *what* he felt for his other Maureen, he knew only that he could not do without her. He loved his own wife, he knew that, and wrote her letters telling her what a perfect wife and perfect woman she had been, and always would be, for him. They had a great marriage, a great relationship. Their marriage did not deserve what he was doing to it. (Although Maureen has the letters, and treasures them still, they were a poor substitute, she feels, for the lovemaking that had ceased.)

Finally, in desperation, Syd asked Maureen to meet his other Maureen. He hoped that his wife would get rid of her for him. Maureen had made up her mind that she would divorce, but this other Maureen sounded 'such a terrible woman' that she felt she owed it to Syd to help him to extricate himself. The other Maureen was a 'common little tart', and would make Syd into a 'laughing stock among his friends and colleagues'. She knew this because Syd had told her so. Thus did the triangle meet for a drink. It turned out that the other Maureen did not believe that Syd's wife was willing to allow the affair to continue; she had believed that Syd wanted out only because his wife was 'putting the screws on'. She had come to the meeting in order to ask Syd's wife to share him with her. She told Maureen that if she'd 'been so bloody marvellous herself' none of this would have happened anyway.

The photograph that Maureen had found, Syd insisted, did not really flatter his girlfriend. His own wife was attractive, but he warned her not to be too hurt when she saw what a beautiful, lovely woman the other Maureen was. But the other Maureen was far from beautiful, far from lovely, she was badly dressed, and 'nothing matched'. She wasn't ugly, wasn't ordinary, just a 'flashy, sexy, dyed blonde'. Maureen explained that she was not standing in Syd's way, and now that she'd met her, Syd was even more welcome to her. She was really angry with him now that she had seen the Other Woman with her own eyes. But no matter how angry she was, she still felt that Syd deserved something better than what he'd found. Syd wanted to break it off with her because he didn't want her. Syd had told her that himself, she hadn't believed him: but, as his wife, she was now confirming what he had so often told her himself. Hearing this the other

Maureen raised her voice, which was in any case harsh, and began shrieking obscenities at the perfectly groomed, perfectly contained, perfectly quiet wife who faced her. The wife stood up, suggested leaving, began walking out. The husband followed, and out on the pavement, the two ran, as if for their lives.

Later that evening, Syd remembered that he had not paid for the drinks. He believed that it was the best thing that had happened to him, seeing his wife and his girlfriend together like that, at close range. He had seen his madness, confronted it, and believed himself to be cured. His wife, however, has not recovered; she still loves her husband, but feels destroyed, and though five months have passed, thinks of divorce, and sometimes (though her husband doesn't know this) even of suicide. There is no cure, she insists, for betrayal. Syd thinks the whole thing is tragic.

However preferable it may be to defeat, Maureen's is a hollow victory. They have made love, but 'something' in Maureen 'is dead'. Maureen had a great marriage (and, as she says, she has the letters to prove it) and Syd had a great marriage (after all he wrote the letters). This is an example of a strong marriage made weaker by the Other Woman.

Handling the crisis successfully does not always mean an unconditional victory. Both Maureen's and Claire's (see Chapter 3) victories were won at great personal cost. Unconditional love demands unqualified sacrifice.

5

Leaving, returning, grieving

Leaving the marital home, even when the home is strifetorn, is, to say the least, a traumatic moment. Those husbands who leave a happy, or seemingly happy, household are all but torn apart by their own action; and their suffering, though real and intense, heightens their sense of 'dramatic destiny' (as one husband put it) and further authenticates the needfulness of their new love. The wife who has been taken unawares is bewildered or, worse, unbalanced and undone, not least by the thought that his final reunion with the Other Woman simultaneously seals his final severing from her. 'There we were, the kids and me all huddled together, sobbing, and there he was, *celebrating* with *her*. Making love with *her*. The thought made me vomit!' said one woman, mother of three.

Pauline and Michael Henderson had been married for six years when she unsuspectingly answered the door to Margaret Spencer, a younger woman with whom she was barely acquainted. Michael had met her at the pub. Surprised, but none the less welcoming, Pauline invited Margaret in for a cup of coffee. The conversation was halting, but the bustle of two small children covered the silences. Increasingly aware of Margaret's distress – she seemed troubled yet excited – Pauline asked her if anything was wrong, and offered to help if she could. That was when Margaret handed over

Michael's letter. Pauline's disbelieving eyes followed the words and she understood that Michael wanted her to pack his things, he'd send her £70 every week, he was going to live with Margaret, he was sorry, but he had been hopelessly in love with her for six months. Stunned and numbed, as if she'd emerged from a collision, though quite unable to speak, she rose from the table, gathered up the two children, and proceeded to take Michael's clothes from the cupboards. Margaret, meanwhile, obligingly fetched suitcases from her car.

The following five or so sleepless days and nights passed in a haze. Pauline now recalls having fed her children, Mike and Pat, on powdered milk and canned food. Almost worse than Michael's desertion was the torment of not having had the vaguest suspicion that anything was amiss. Michael's job as chauffeur to a neurotic, irascible managing director of a group of companies that were going through hard times in the recession was, she thought, the cause of his later nights and increased moodiness. Michael was often required to drive his employer at night. She'd never met him, but she had hated him, and tried to make her husband's life at home as comfortable as possible. She was angry with herself, ashamed of herself, and could not forgive herself for her blind trustingness. She spent all her rage on herself, there was none left for Michael or even Margaret. She had failed to guess, and the consequence of that was a failed marriage and a broken home for her children.

Howard and Clare Siddons had been married for eighteen years, and had two children aged 16 and 13. A miscarriage eight years earlier had prompted Howard to have a vasectomy. Howard was a contracts manager for a carpet company and hoped to be made a director. Clare openly enjoyed her home and family. She took great pride in his work and in him, and served on the school PTA.

When Howard had told her months earlier that there would be extra meetings after hours, Clare had believed him. For Howard had long had a rival contender for the Board,

Rex Crowe, and Clare knew that Rex would require a great deal of outmanoeuvring. Rex had a difficult, demanding wife who sabotaged him. Clare went out of her way to show Howard how lucky he was not to have a wife like Rex's. But for all Clare's support, the strain she believed to be work stress began to tell. Howard looked ill, lost weight, and Clare suspected an ulcer. She had made an appointment with their GP.

When Howard came home after a meeting, at around 10 or 11 p.m., Clare would always wait up for him in their bed. She would prepare his cocoa in the thermos and place it on the bedside table. One night Howard came home earlier than he had said he would, at about 11 p.m. He was gaunt and pale. He would usually undress as soon as he came home, but while still wearing his suit, he sat on the edge of their bed, covered his face with his hands, and burst into tears. Clare thought he was ill, fetched a glass of water and tried to comfort him, and wanted to call the doctor, assuring him all the while it didn't matter that Rex Crowe had got the directorship.

At first, Howard did not tell her of Sarah. Angrily he told her he had other problems. Clare asked him what he meant. He told her he was in love with Sarah. Clare knew her, she was Howard's secretary, 28 and mother of 3-year-old twin girls. Clare ran out of the room – to vomit. Normally Howard would have helped her, but he left her alone. When Clare returned to the room, Howard told her that it had been going on for six months, that for the last three months he had been trying to stall Sarah, but she had forced him to choose. He had promised her he would be at her flat for breakfast. He'd got that directorship a week previously. He and Sarah had been certain she knew about them. Because how can you live with a man and not know? A woman can tell when her man has switched off. Clare felt it was not Howard who spoke and whom she heard, but Sarah.

Howard kept repeating that he was hopelessly in love. He left and kept his promise to Sarah. All that happened eighteen months ago. Howard sees his own children irregularly. He has cancelled at least six Saturday appointments with them. An ulcer has been diagnosed. Clare has agreed to divorce, but still hopes he will come back to her. She is convinced that things went so far because she was 'stupidly trusting'. She believes Howard was 'seduced', and blames Sarah.

There are husbands who defect after days, weeks, months and even years of discussion, negotiation, counter-negotiation and promises. Some leave only when the last excuse has become invalid – perhaps young Jonathan, the last of four children, has finally passed his A-levels. But, strangest of all, perhaps, are those husbands who have preserved a meaningful, deep and full relationship with their wives, even though certain arranged times are given over to the Other Woman, and then, after some years, leave sometimes for the constant Other Woman in their lives and sometimes for a newer one.

Some husbands leave sneakily, taking their clothes while the wife is at work or out of the house, because they are too cowardly to tell their wife face-to-face of their intentions. Some leave the traditional 'Dear Jane' letter. Some telephone after they have left, and some contact a friend or relative, such as a parent, to ask them to tell her. Other husbands confide in adolescent or older sons or daughters and transfer the pain of breaking such heart-breaking news to them. Those husbands who are able to bring themselves to face their wives with what they are about to do, usually on that very day, often do so in floods of tears at the hurt they are causing. And there are even those husbands who ask, or allow, the Other Woman in their lives to call their wives to explain and inform them of their fate. Some husbands, afraid of being dissuaded from leaving, go to the length of bringing the Other Woman with them, to force a confrontation with his wife, and sometimes to help him pack his bags. And there are some husbands who walk out and away and are never seen again, though, occasionally they are found by private detectives or the Salvation Army or some other similar agency. A curt letter from a solicitor while the husband is away on a business trip is yet another way of imparting the news to an unsuspecting wife.

Not a few husbands are deceived into believing they will be defecting from a wholly unsuspecting wife. These are the wives who have refused to 'let on', hoping the Other Woman is a passing fancy. That the husband may only be confirming what is already too well known, and perhaps even documented, does little to alleviate his wife's utter desolation. Needless to say, those wives who had no notion of their husband's double life were those who blamed themselves even more acutely for his desertion.

Many husbands, however, return. Some would return to the family but lack the courage, or are too ashamed, or too proud to admit that they have made a mistake. Some beg to return and are refused, and find new locks turned against them. After seven weeks with the Other Woman in his life, Gerald, 52, a furniture salesman, decided to surprise his wife and returned while she was out at work. But the locks had been changed. Furious, he left. He said he couldn't understand how his wife could have done such a thing.

The patterns of return frequently cause more heartbreak and confusion than the original desertion. Sometimes a husband sneaks away from the Other Woman to spend an afternoon or morning with his wife, often in bed, usually leaving some hope for a more permanent return. Many wives speak of recurring sexual fantasies of beginning an affair with their own husbands, and sometimes wives liberated from prior constraints, and fired by the vigour of sexual competition, surprise and confuse their husbands with their new and unbridled ardour. Sometimes these afternoons, mornings or lunch breaks achieve the intensity of a long-lost or unknown ecstasy, and many a deserted wife has seduced her husband back home again, often more out of a desire to wound the Other Woman than out of love for her husband. But whatever the motivating factor, the results are far-ranging, often unsettling, and sometimes destructive to everyone, especially when the husband confesses his infidelity to the Other Woman. Those husbands who know they are the vehicle by which the two women in his life seek to 'get at' one another are not above exploiting this weakness, even to the point of snidely setting the one against the other, usually by making some oblique reference to one or the other's failings.

And then there are those men who return for no more than a good meal. Often they look hungry and uncared for, even ill, and return to their wives as if to their mothers. Surprisingly few wives reported any sense of satisfaction at seeing their defected husbands thus reduced. Many were very concerned for their physical welfare. They acknowledged that the hope of a permanent return was deeply unsettling to everyone and did little to help the adjustment process, particularly when the husband stayed for a few days or even weeks at a time. Apart from the need for a good meal, some husbands return to tell their wives of the promotion they've received, or the prize they were awarded at work for achieving the most sales, while others come for a shoulder to cry on; they've been made redundant, or did not get their promotion and are too embarrassed and too ashamed to tell their Other Woman.

These men who return, temporarily, for a few hours, often behave like a husband while making it abundantly clear that while some husbandly obligations and even privileges remain, others do not. The core may have gone from the relationship, but he has not entirely released himself from his commitment, and so spreads it, like a thin, almost useless blanket, over both women. By seeing his wife, even sleeping with her, though living with the Other Woman, he consolidates his illusion of freedom. In a sense, then, his wife represents his permissible freedom. In these circumstances where the Other Woman had claimed to understand his obligations to see his former wife, there is little, without laying herself open to charges of extreme heartlessness, that she can do to alter his behaviour. It would be too risky to prohibit him from having any contact whatsoever with his wife. (The Other Woman dare not behave like a wife – that would be the one sure way to lose him to his wife; besides, that is one accusation that she cannot endure.)

Steve Truswell was one of those husbands who, like Howard Siddons, informed his wife of twenty-two years, Vicky, that he would be leaving her the next morning for Emma Sanderson, a secretary whom he'd met while attending a pharmaceutical conference in Denmark. Though Steve wept and Vicky howled, Steve left anyway – but not before packing two suitcases – because he could not let Emma down. It turned out that Steve had applied for, and been granted, a two-month study fellowship in Switzerland. He was taking Emma with him, and proudly showed her Emma's photograph. The company would be sending Vicky half his salary, and he'd attend to all the necessary financial arrangements when he returned. He'd seen a solicitor who'd offered to find one for Vicky to act for her.

Vicky spent the following days going over the marriage, puzzling over where she had gone wrong, castigating herself for not having guessed that their lives were about to be shattered. Their boys, 12 and 14, were away at school, and she had a three-mornings-a-week job as a medical secretary. Steve was a research chemist who had seemed happy enough to be in the marketing division of the largest drug company in the world. An amiable creature of habit, he had seemed content enough and secure. What their sex lives lacked in quantity was made up in quality. Vicky saw herself as a fulfilled woman – Steve had been rather more attentive recently. Again and again her mind returned to Emma, a chemistry graduate who, poor girl, had been forced into accepting a job as a secretary. *That* burned: Vicky had never been to university.

She expected Steve to telephone, but he did not. She found she couldn't stop eating. After four days of silence and sleeplessness to the point of madness, she telephoned his office and asked to speak to Emma Sanderson, and when she was put through, hung up; she found she couldn't speak. A little while later she telephoned again; this time she asked to speak to her husband. He sounded cold and impatient when she spoke to him. He said, 'We will be leaving for Switzerland in ten days,' and added that she'd hear from his solicitors before then. It was the use of the word 'we' that undid Vicky, as it undoes so many wives.

Vicky's ice-cold paralysis of disbelief ended, and in its stead she was overpowered by a furious despair. She rushed to the bathroom, tempted to take every tablet she could find and, opening cupboards, was confronted by Steve's seemingly endless collection of after-shave lotions and colognes that she now felt should have alerted her in the first place. In a frenzy over what she had failed to see, she began dashing the bottles to the tiled floor, and then, when there were no more bottles, she grabbed a pair of large scissors, raced to Steve's cupboards and systematically cut up all his best clothes. Not satisfied, she grabbed his suitcases, threw the pieces in, added some of the jagged glass from the bathroom, telephoned the taxi company Steve used and sent the suitcases to him, to be paid for at the other end. After that, exhausted, she fell asleep.

The time sequence is still muddled in Vicky's mind. That she has no idea how long she slept hardly matters, now. She was awakened by Steve's desperate entreaty. '*Tell me you're alive! Tell me you're alive!*'

Steve later told her that the broken glass in the suitcases had driven him to believe that she had 'committed suicide while the balance of her mind was disturbed.' He framed his thoughts in this very phrase; and realized, as he put it, that '*he* might be deprived of *his* wife.' He'd been certain that, no matter what happened, she would always be there, for him.

This is another example of a wife who says she doesn't know whether or not she meant to shock her husband back to his senses. She can't say why she behaved as she did – and she's not the sort who loses her temper. It may or may not have been a desperate and final ploy. Certainly Emma believes the jagged glass was deliberately put in the suitcase as a ruse to get Steve back. Vicky knows this because Steve told her after they were reconciled.

When the break has been made final, the defeated wife often finds to her astonishment that she is expected to behave like a good loser. She is expected to take defeat well, and to step aside for the victor, as if she'd been running in a marathon and only just been pipped at the post. When she does not take it well, but grieves instead, she is said to be as spiteful and as difficult as all scorned women. (One wonders, are there no scorned men? We hear only of a woman scorned.) Much has been made of the fact that there are no mourning rites for the death of a marriage, even when the death blow was not struck by a third person. The good loser principle means that the grief that is rejection is almost an illegitimate grief. The defeated wife is expected to 'get on with it', to 'pull herself together and stop being so paranoid'. That another woman's glory is being built upon her ashes is not her business; it has nothing to do with her.

Perhaps this comment from a victorious wife will shed some light on the grief factor within the Woman versus Woman conflict. Sally is a market consultant, a highly practical and unusually pretty woman of about 35. 'At the time I felt that I would have rather had to face cancer than the Other Woman. Cancer, you see, is nobody's fault.' That is how Sally felt while the conflict raged.

Sally now says that she does not altogether regret the experience, though of course she wishes that she had not been called upon to endure it.

> 'I found out a lot about myself, about the basics of being a woman. You see, no man could have responded to the Other Man in anything like the way I, being a woman, responded. In a way I felt timeless and ancient – primeval, I suppose. I was called upon to protect my family and

myself – our survival depended on me. I knew we might lose, but by God, I was determined to do my best not to!'

What Sally meant about the basics of being a woman was keeping her man, keeping the family together and intact. She was not going to fall into what she saw as the Other Woman's trap of the 'ungovernable anger of a jilted wife'. Up until then she had always believed that she wouldn't and couldn't try to hold on to a man who didn't want her. She had too much pride, she believed, for that. She says she learned that there is more pride in self-defence than in retreat.

Sylvia's eleven-year marriage ended when her industrialist husband, Keith, left her for the Other Woman, who was thirty years younger than he and twenty years younger than his wife. It was Sylvia's second marriage and Keith's third. Sylvia's first marriage had ended after eighteen years when her husband died. It had been an unusually happy marriage. 'When Colin died, everyone came to hold my hand,' she said. For months her house had been filled with sympathizers who offered encouragement as well as support. Even the lawyers went out of their way to be kind. She found the death of a marriage very different and much harder to bear than the death of a husband. After Keith left, those few remaining friends who did not drop her were impatient with her. The lawyers were openly forbearing and impersonal. Scorned by a man, she felt she was also being scorned by the world. People told her 'it's not a tragedy, you're an attractive, vital woman so you'll find someone else.' Her children took the same view. But she wants her own husband. Keith's children were made to choose between Sylvia and the 'new popsie'. They chose the latter. Twelve effortful years had resulted in nothing; she had worked hard at her relationship with her stepchildren. Bereft of them now, she grieves over the wasted years. She longs to hate Keith, but cannot. Instead she hates the 'popsie' whose name is unmentionable. She is convinced she handled things badly; self-blame is tacked on to the grief. She and Keith never had a child together. She tortures herself with the thought that Keith will become a father again, at 62. She hopes something will be wrong with this unborn child, wishes it to be a mongol. . . . (Keith had been impotent with her. . . .) The image of the 'popsie' never leaves her mind. Keith now refuses to speak to her children although they looked upon him as a father.

Sylvia is an occupational therapist and therefore a career is open to her. But she is apathetic, depressed, in grief, and has nothing to get up for in the mornings. She is on a diet of valium and whisky, even though Keith has been gone for two years. She feels there is *no* comparison between what she is going through now and what she went through when her previous husband died. However much she hates to admit it, the truth is that the death of her first husband was 'better' for her than this, because when he died, his death could only be blamed on God and not on herself, and certainly not on another woman. A widow is the continuation of a wife, because in her view marriage, like life, can only be ended by real death. She will love her husband until her death, but she would rather lose him to death than to another woman. She could endure widowhood, but not divorce. An ex-wife means an ex-life which, after all, is a fate worse than death.

Dionne went against everyone's wishes when she married Tom. They had five children in six years, one of whom was a spastic. Dionne's father was a stockbroker, Tom's a coal-miner. When they met Tom was an out-of-work actor. Dionne, who had been to RADA, believed in his talent far more than she believed in her own. She made his career, and the management of it, her own career. Success piled upon success. Tom became a film star of international acclaim.

Dionne never quite accepted the Other Woman in his life, though from the outset she pretended to trust him, pretended to believe every lie, every excuse. 'I knew that when he stopped lying, when he no longer had the need to lie, that I would be in deep shit. . . .'

She adored her husband and gloried in the success to which she had contributed so much. True, at 32 she became obsessed with her looks, and spent hours mourning each sign of each new wrinkle; her close girlfriends grew used to the magnifying mirror on the coffee table, grew used to examining her face with her, but sympathized, giving reassurance. They pitied her, but understood; she poured out her terrors as she poured the coffee, and was consoled as well as encouraged by their advice and their sympathy. Again and again she would say, 'As long as he lies to me I'll be OK.'

When Tom used to return from a trip, or spend more time with the family, Dionne was as radiant as a first-time bride. The house was filled with creative, trendy, important people – truly it was *La Dolce Vita*; the children were included, and Tom was the stern father, the devoted husband.

It is now eight years since Tom died. He died seventeen years after they had been married, when he was 47 and Dionne was 43. His illness lasted two years, and 'we both knew that he was going to die, but we were in it *together*. It was terrible. But the pain, for me, couldn't be compared to the other pain, the jealousy, the terror of another woman taking him away from me.'

6

Recruiting the Other Woman

Some wives consciously contrive to bring the Other Woman into their husband's life. There are several different categories of this kind of reaction. They see the Other Woman as useful, so useful in fact that if she doesn't exist, she must be created. So they seek her out diligently. For the Other Woman can be just the right sort of stimulant to a stale marriage, provoking a charge of adrenalin for both husband and wife.

In the following cases the wife was concerned to make the Other Woman the casualty of her husband's ecstasy.

Margaret Marshall always knew when her husband, Jonathan, had ended an affair because that was when he got nasty. They have now been married for twenty-nine years; the pattern began about twenty years ago. Margaret had grown used to the advantages that go with being the wife of a commodity broker. Jonathan is 'difficult and temperamental' but Margaret is used to that, too. None of their three children live at home. For business reasons, the Marshalls often entertain. Margaret makes it *her* business to invite as many lovely young candidates as she can find, as often as it is necessary. Jonathan's better mood and extra generosity mark the beginning of his new affair. This way, Margaret feels, the wheels keep turning, which is 'probably best for everyone and certainly better than a divorce'. Margaret is as convinced as it is ever possible to be that 'Jonathan will never leave, because if he did, he would no longer have his freedom. Jonathan has the best of both worlds, and I have the lesser of two evils.'

Financial considerations are frequently a disincentive to divorce, even when the marriage is miserable, and even when there is no shortage of money. Lisa, for example, was convinced that but for financial considerations her husband, Gerald, would have been delighted to divorce her. They had two children and a fourteen-year-old marriage. Gerald had started out as a small manufacturer of jeans, the business flourished, and though Lisa did not go to the factory, her acumen, as well as her excellence as a hostess, contributed in no small measure to his success. Though the marriage had been anything but a success, Gerald's business triumphs meant that a divorce would be too costly to contemplate; it would mean losing one-third of his assets to Lisa. Therefore Lisa determined that the only way to get Gerald to want her to resign as his wife was if a suitable incentive could be found. In other words, he would have to want to get rid of her so much, that he would be willing to pay for her to go. He would have to fall passionately in love. She knew her husband well enough to know what sort of girl could do the trick. Gerald was a born snob, but had so far not managed to meet the kind of people he regarded as the right sort. He wanted a classy (public school), well-made (looking like a model) and new (young) girl. This combination would go well with his Porsche. Lisa set about finding the right sort of girl. Gerald's burgeoning business needed a directors' dining room and Lisa undertook its organization. She acquired, along with the right china, a 19-year-old trendy, a graceful, qualified *cordon bleu* cook called Miranda. She treated her as if she were a daughter being coached how to please, how to humour, a father. Miranda turned out to be a gifted pupil. Much as it hurt, Gerald parted with one-third of his assets, which from Lisa's point of view was altogether fair, though less than she deserved.

Several wives went to war with the objective of keeping the Other Woman at bay until a suitable replacement husband could be found. Few revealed to their husbands their real reason for wanting to continue with the marriage. (The only wife who was absolutely honest when she told her husband about why she wanted to stay married was not believed.) The theory was that it would be easier to find someone else whilst still under the protective umbrella of a marriage. They held this view for several reasons: their married status made them less available therefore more desirable, and apparently safer than a divorcée; they would be less obvious about their search for a new man; they would not be blackballed by other wives.

'I literally begged my husband not to leave me,' said Andrea Longman, 31, who had two children aged 5 and 3, and had been married for seven years.

> 'I begged for another chance. I told him I was ready to agree to anything – he could live with her, spend whole nights with her – begged only for the chance to get used to the idea of being divorced. And I implored him not to tell anyone – not his parents, not mine, no one. I swore I wouldn't nag him, wouldn't ask questions. All I wanted was to know which nights were hers and which were mine. He was still sleeping with me. On her nights I went to night classes in photography – that was how I met Jim.
>
> 'Eventually I told Jim a bit about her, about Marianne, but he was convinced my husband would only leave me if I left him. He persuaded me to get out! Jim was a 35-year-old bachelor. I think, in fact I'm sure, he wouldn't have looked at me if I'd been single. He really didn't want to get married, you see.'

A husband sometimes leaves his family because he cannot bear living with his wife, and for no other reason. When it is clear that her husband left her to escape her, she invents a mythical Other Woman and afterwards claims that he left her because of her.

Terry's wife Lois left him after a seven-year marriage because he had 'financial difficulties, was a fool about money, and drank too much'. Their mutual friends, even those who took Lois's side, did not consider these factors to be sufficient grounds for walking out on him. However, as Terry remarked, 'if another woman could be brought into the story, it made Lisa's argument of her case much more reasonable.' She therefore put the story about that Terry's second wife, whom he only met *after* Lois had left, was the real cause of the divorce. Terry discovered this when one of their mutual friends wrote declining an invitation to his wedding party because Terry 'surely ought to have had the sensitivity to appreciate that in the circumstances he couldn't come.' This puzzled Terry until some months later it emerged that Lois had said that the real reason for her leaving had been Bess, Terry's new wife. When Terry was able to talk to Lois about it she confirmed that she had said these things about Bess, but offered to correct the impression she admitted she had deliberately put out.

It seems too that there is no more effective a shield from a husband's unwelcome sexual needs than the Other Woman. Sally, a former secretary, liked her husband but didn't like sex. She had never liked it much; as far as she was concerned, sex had always been an overrated pastime. She'd had two children, and ten years previously when the second was born, Sally 'went off sex altogether.' She put up with it when she had to, and 'faked it.' Her husband Jake, a bus conductor, had always had an eye for a pretty girl, and many a pretty girl was befriended by Sally. She knew what was going on, but affected total ignorance. Sally owes infrequent sex, three or four times a year for the past ten years, and a friendly, peaceful marriage to Other Women.

Sally's attitude in the late twentieth century is not too dissimilar from Mrs Boswell's attitude in the late eighteenth century. Mrs Boswell advised her husband to take concubines because her sexual appetite was not as high as his, and because of the fear of pregnancy. That particular fear is not as real for Sally as it was for Mrs Boswell (it should be remembered that *no* form of contraception is 100 per cent baby-proof), but it is clear that both Sally and Mrs Boswell had lower sex drives than their husbands. But although twentieth-century, or post-Freudian, society is noted for its indiscriminate use of candour, Sally, unlike Mrs Boswell, has to contend with the easy option of divorce. Marriages were terminated in former times by death rather than by divorce. Mrs Boswell could afford to suggest concubines; Sally arranges and permits concubines of a sort, but deploys silence in order to do so.

'In a way it was like arranging a marriage, being a marriage-broker, finding someone who was much better suited to Stuart than I was,' said Lucy Beach, 28, of her husband Stuart to whom she had been married for four years. Divorce proceedings began when the only child of the marriage, Diana, was 3.

> 'I think I knew it had all been a ghastly mistake when Diana was only six months old. It was a terrible situation because Stuart was such a nice man! You could say he was every girl's dream – a corporate lawyer, handsome, intelligent, kind with a fair sense of humour. He was the perfect husband – a girl couldn't ask for more! But the thought of living with him for the rest of my life was something I couldn't face. I couldn't face the thought of hurting him either – he didn't deserve it. I was moody and depressed and he was tolerant. He was keen on bridge and I hated card games – he loved gardening and I hated living in the suburbs. The sex was OK – the earth didn't move, but that was OK. I didn't have anyone else – I just didn't want to be married to him.
>
> 'I used to daydream about him finding someone else, even though I knew he wasn't the type. I still can't decide whether I contrived it all or not, but he had a secretary

called Theresa, who could play bridge and loved growing vegetables. She was a nice girl, not too attractive, but she made the best of herself. She was 22, but was the sort of girl who had been ready for marriage since she was 10. Sometimes she took my place at bridge – I'd arrange it. Stuart went to see her parents' vegetables. . . . I don't know how long it took them to jump into bed, but after about four months Stuart asked for a divorce. He was most apologetic. Theresa never guessed what I'd been up to. We see each other sometimes because of Diana. Theresa's always perfectly polite, but she makes it very clear that she'd rather not see me. As for me – well, my conscience is clear, which is more than Theresa can say of hers! The main thing is that Stuart wasn't hurt.'

It would seem that in this case the Other Woman was an almost magical conscience-salver for the wife.

Giles and Beth Sanderson have been married for eleven years; it is the second marriage for both. Beth was widowed after an eighteen-year marriage and Giles was divorced after a three-year postwar mistake of a marriage. They have four children (two each), all married. Beth is 52, Giles is 60.

When Beth married Giles she was a 40-year-old widow whose marital expectations were based on the 'tolerant, accepting authority' of her previous happy marriage. Giles's three-year marriage produced two children and was unremarkable even in its unhappiness, and so left few memories of any sort. He had several liaisons, spread over twenty years, of varying durations up until the time of his marriage to Beth and, as he himself says, has never been happier, more content or more at ease with anyone in his life. He's very affectionate and 'we fall asleep with our arms around one another.' Nor has his affectionateness decreased even though, for the past five years, he has

'not been able to make love to me. I've given this enormous thought, as you can imagine, and I've come to the

> conclusion that it is the Madonna-whore complex. As long as I'm his wife he can't make love to me. It is, of course, hurtful, deeply hurtful. He would like to make love to me, but he can't, or he would *not* like to, and so he can't. It may change, or it may not. I don't know. We've talked about it, a bit, not too much. He may be right – at least that's what I tell myself. He's not keen on going to one of those so-called sexologists and nor, quite frankly, am I. I'm not fat, I'm not thin – I'm just neat. I'm not very attractive but then I'm not unattractive either. I've got no hang-ups – I don't call being able to do without sex a hang-up, certainly not at 52. I've come to terms with it.'

Though celibacy represents no real hardship to her, Beth sees no reason why Giles should react in the same way. 'Sex has different connotations for men, after all, there's no point in rebelling against nature.' Beth's tolerance, however, stopped short at prostitution. They had a mutual friend, a divorcée called Jeanine, who coped very well with her life. Beth thought, why not? – but was silent. Once or twice she asked Giles to call on Jeanine and collect her diary or her sunglasses and occasionally to deliver a book or a few biscuits she'd baked – Jeanine's favourites.

When she was sure her plan had been consummated she waited for Giles's confession. ('Of course I knew he'd tell me about it – he tells me everything!') She handled the confession with her customary tact, her customary compassion and then added a confession or two of her own: false pride and vanity, which meant that she could forgive everyone anything and everything; he was welcome to continue with Jeanine as long as he liked, on condition that Jeanine would never be told that she knew anything about it.

Beth's reasoning, she says, is very simple. She would have been humiliated if Jeanine knew that she knew. Besides, this way she and Giles would both be engaged in deception of the same description, deception which was their own, very intimate, secret. (But could this not also have been a highly gratifying form of generalship on Beth's part? After all, Jeanine's affair was due to Beth's manoeuvre.)

Speaking of her former husband of fifteen years, Brenda said,

> 'But you must understand that this man's love for me was manic. I'm not saying it because I am beautiful or anything else, but it was a known fact. You can go round and if you say do you know Ken Williams and Brenda, people will tell you it's the biggest shock they've ever had in their lives. When it happened all my friends assessed their marriages and suddenly drew in their horns and said "my God, they're the one couple we thought it would never happen to." We're the beautiful people, the ones everybody copied. But this wasn't an act, it was true.'

Ken had left her for Ingrid. When Brenda married him, Ken had a rare disease of the muscles; Brenda says she built him up from a skeleton to 'a very powerful human being'. But now 'he looks like a broken man, he's very bent and very white.' She asked him to 'stay, go through your affair. Stay for your children's sake, not for mine. Have your affair, but pretend to be at home.'

Their sex lives had been active, experimental, rewarding; they had made passionate love the night before he left to go to Ingrid. But Ken had wanted a more unorthodox sexual life with his wife; he had wanted to have his wife and another woman in bed at the same time. Brenda could not bring herself to accept this. Ken had taken photographs of her in the nude, in erotic postures. She had consented to that, reluctantly; she didn't see how she could consent to more: 'His erotic ideas clashed with mine, and I didn't begin to guess how important this was to him.' Brenda recalls everything about the night they met Ingrid whom she thought was a most unpleasant character. 'I had been the apple of my husband's eye; I was far too self-assured, I never ever thought he would look at anybody else.'

Ingrid, however, had none of Brenda's qualms. From the beginning her affair with Ken had included other women. Ken told Brenda that Ingrid was a woman of 'sophisticated sexual tastes'. Ingrid had been more than willing to find other women for him. Ken and Ingrid have now been married for two years, and it would seem that the practice continues. Brenda has heard this from two of the women who joined in and, besides, her children have told her about the kinds of women who are in their father's home so often.

Ingrid, like Sally, is an example of a wife who is prepared to recruit Other Women for her husband for sexual purposes. Sally is less sophisticated, and therefore more discreet.

The role of Other Woman is one that Phyllis plays well and often. She is 50 but looks about 38; she is an intelligent, articulate woman, a highly successful insurance broker. Her belief that all her life her extraordinary beauty has been her great asset has endowed her with an unusual level of self-confidence. Her high cheekbones highlight the absolute oval of her face, the perfect proportions of her miraculously chiselled nose, the shape and softness of her huge blue eyes compel the attention of everyone who sees her. She was married briefly, and then divorced. One marriage was more than enough. She has had 'at least eight long-term and important relationships with married men'.

Her current married man, Brad, a financier, is 58, as is his wife, Muriel.

> 'Brad's wife knows about me, though she never says anything. I met him eight years ago, and I enjoy him. I enjoy going round the world with him. I can yell at him if I like. I feel equal with him. It's a good feeling. He calls Muriel from every airport, though he lies about which airport it is. He calls her all the time – at any hour, several times a day. He goes wild if she's not there, so she's always at home. She's his security blanket. I call him, too, whenever I like. He encourages me. But we can't really

talk – he can't tell me he loves me – there are phones in every room and they light up, so Muriel knows when he's on the phone, and listens in. He bought a phone for the garden and phones me from there sometimes, and she knows about that, but lets him do it. It amuses me, but not in the sense of being funny. I've got my own way of looking at things; you have to be pretty sophisticated to be like that. Brad is fun to be with. If I were married to him, I'd never believe him. I don't try to take husbands away – any more.

'I could, and I would, if it suited me, recruit the Other Woman. I think the reason Muriel likes me is that if she could have recruited me I would have been the woman she wanted. I keep her husband in order. I keep him from gambling, from doing a lot of things he would do, so why not?

'If I were on the other side I'd recruit someone like me. I mean, if I had a husband who needed to have that Other Woman in his life. It's not that men need a change, it's just that something's missing that needs to be filled, another dimension, perhaps, or another point of view. It goes over after a while, but if the woman (i.e. the wife) on the other side is hysterical she will keep the affair going for ever. This is the problem that a lot of women do not understand. Because, basically, I don't think that men want to break up their marriage. A clever wife can stop it – though an affair might last for ever. If he comes back to a contented home, why should he want to leave?

'Brad is not the sort of man I would want to marry. There's no tension between us because of this. But he'll probably be in my life until I die, and I'll be in his life until the day he dies. Of course, if he were free, I would marry him. . . . Sometimes I fly off with another man – why shouldn't I? – and his wife phones me – she finds me wherever I am – and tells me that he's very unhappy, very miserable – she can't do a thing with him – he's gambling wildly, taking out young girls and hating it. But she never asks me to come back, never openly admits that she knows I'm his mistress. She's just a home body, a slave to her husband. I know about the young girls. Brad hates it, and I hate it, so I usually call him after one of Muriel's phone calls, and we get together again.

'I know Brad needs his wife more than he needs me. She's too clever to force him to choose. She uses me to control him. I put up with it because it suits me. His kids know about me. I've met them. Look, the whole thing works, for all of us. He's a man I can *rely* on. When I was ill he got me to the best doctors.'

Phyllis sees herself as one of the sophisticates of this world. She concedes, somewhat reluctantly, that Brad's wife, Muriel, could be hurt by the whole arrangement, but then that is an 'occupational hazard' common to all wives. If his wife is his security blanket, is it not possible that his Other Woman is his wet-nurse? But Phyllis accepted even this rather unpleasant analogy. 'It suits me,' she insisted. 'It suits all of us.'

She pointed out that Brad *never* gives her presents. Air tickets and hotel accommodation (always first-class) are on the business. Once she had to lend him quite a large sum of money, several thousand dollars. Though Muriel is not in the business, she has signing powers. Phyllis's presents, however, come from Muriel – quite large cheques are deposited in her account. Phyllis declined to specify the amounts.

It may be that Muriel considers the cost of Phyllis on the payroll more economical than a divorce would be. At any rate, it would appear that Muriel is ready to pay Phyllis to keep her marriage running, much in the way she would be ready to pay a housekeeper, or for that matter, any hired hand, to keep her household running.

Whether the Other Woman was recruited to prop up a marriage or to break one down, she was none the less used by the wife. The awareness of having been used usually comes too late, and many a second wife regrets not having met or at least seen through the wife. But few Other Women greet the knowledge of their recruitment with the same degree of 'sophistication' as Phyllis.

7

Children and the ways of sabotage

In the Woman versus Woman conflict children play a significant and sometimes dangerous role, ranging from direct to indirect intervention. For the Other Woman they are adversaries to be overcome or won over. For the wife they are allies whose deployment varies from saboteur to diplomat, and for the husband they are the representatives of his conscience or the permanent remnants of a former life that refuses to vanish into limbo like a marriage. The relationship between the parent and the child is crucial to the stance the child will adopt, and in some instances the triangle of father-daughter versus mother existed long before the advent of the Other Woman. Most commonly, however, children side with their mother against the Other Woman, and there are even cases where the children have known about the Other Woman but kept their information secret from their mother, made their own independent investigations and acted accordingly.

Sharon had always been a popular, confident child; other girls feared and respected her, yet coveted her company. Teachers relied on her; she was good at games and conscientious over her studies, but not brilliant or original or anything remotely as discomfiting as that. She obeyed the rules and made sure everyone else did, too. She was a tidy girl and, at 16, as neat on the page as she was in her appearance. She was aware that among her contemporaries she was something of a status symbol. A party was not a party if Sharon did not attend. She knew this and was unsurprised – it had always been so.

Her mother was a legal secretary and her father an accounts executive. The family had only one car, but three children. The household was as neat and as orderly as Sharon herself. Soon after Sharon turned 16 things changed. A new name entered the family's vocabulary: 'that Stacey woman' disturbed the peace, echoed through their mother's tears, and penetrated Sharon's dreams. 'That Stacey woman' had a daughter, Amelda, and she and Sharon were in the same class at school. Amelda, tall and fair with sky blue eyes, was prettier than Sharon, but her timidity made her awkward and she was a reluctant loner. Amelda was a few months younger than Sharon, and a birthday party was arranged. Very quietly, though with her usual efficiency, Sharon set about arranging a boycott. No one was to go to that party – no one. Whoever went would never be Sharon's friend. And whoever warned Amelda that no one would turn up would be Sharon's permanent enemy. Because, as Sharon told her friends, Amelda's mother was a 'whore, a common tart'. Amelda's mother was 'that Stacey woman'. And when Amelda's mother phoned, as she was certain to do, to ask where the guests were, each girl would be obliged to say that she wasn't coming 'because *you* know *why*, Mrs Stacey'. Three girls were telephoned and then Mrs Stacey got the message and gave up.

Sharon is now 34, married, and a mother of three daughters. She is still popular, confident, a good organizer, much sought after for committees but safely ordinary-looking. She is not entirely proud of the way she victimized, as she puts it, 'poor Amelda'. She believes she 'behaved badly' but 'can't honestly say' that she really regrets what she did. Her father was 'grim and angry' when he spoke to her about what had happened to 'poor Amelda' but Sharon denied everything and said she wasn't surprised Amelda was putting the blame on her, she wasn't surprised, either, that her father was taking Amelda's side instead of hers.

A few weeks later, probably less than three weeks, Sharon believes now, 'that Stacey woman' disappeared from the family vocabulary. Sharon suspects she frightened the poor woman off – who would have dared deal with a stepdaughter like me, she asks, quite reasonably. The matter was never discussed in Sharon's household again. For all her self-confidence, however, she cannot bring herself to mention a word of this to her father, now a widower, still mourning the wife who died three years ago.

A further example of a daughter engaged in the Woman versus Woman conflict is that of Jennifer, now 22, and a nurse. She was 16, and tumbled to the Other Woman long before her own mother did. Jennifer only told her mother of her suspicions when they had been proven, and then the mother and daughter went into action together, though it was the daughter who took the initiative and planned the strategy.

Jennifer's parents, Dennis and Isobella, had become friendly with a younger couple, Edward and Belinda, because the two men had recently gone into their own estate agency business. (Belinda's father had financed his son-in-law.) From the very beginning Jennifer had disliked her parents' new friend. She disliked her harsh voice, the way she handled her two-year-old son, the way she expected Jennifer to take care of him when she came to visit. It was Jennifer, and not her mother, who noticed the frequency with which Belinda 'forgot' her spectacles and her cigarette lighter, or her diary. 'Why does she come here so often?' she asked her mother. 'She's not your friend. She's not your type. She's too young to be a friend of yours!' But Jennifer's mother said she thought Belinda was lonely.

The two couples appeared to be spending more and more time together. Jennifer's father, Dennis, had always been casual about the state of their amiably run household. Four children and two dogs meant toys and hairs were strewn everywhere. When Dennis came home he, too, liked to shuffle around and relax. In his jeans and a heavy, almost cuddly, sweater and with a pipe cocked at an impish angle, he looked rather like a giant teddy-bear himself. Now, however, he became critical, irritable, and very concerned about the state of his clothes, especially his shirts. He acquired new ties.

It was during this time that Jennifer thought she saw her father and Belinda driving in Belinda's car. But she wasn't sure. She said nothing. About a week later she saw Belinda in her car, alone. Jennifer should have been at school, but had been sent out to buy a single tall rose at a florist. It was to be presented to one of the school dignitaries, who had made an unexpected visit. She raised the rose in greeting and rushed on, and pretended not to hear Belinda's harsh voice call out, 'Why aren't you at school?' She decided, there and then, not to say she'd seen Belinda, but to wait and see whether her father, who had always been Victorian as well as amiable, would want to know why she had been out of school. If he asked her that night, it would mean he would have spoken to Belinda.

That is precisely what happened.

'What were you doing out of school?'

'I wasn't out of school.'

'Don't lie! Someone saw you carrying a rose wrapped in cellophane!'

'Who saw me?'

'Never mind who saw you! What were you doing?'

Jennifer explained what she had been doing.

The next day she came home from school early and told her mother everything and all her fears, all her suspicions, how much she hated Belinda, how much she hated her father, how sad she was for her mother and so on. She told her mother she would go and see Belinda's father. Her mother did not even try to dissuade her, but instead added one or two suggestions of her own. First, they would have to deny – on oath, if necessary, that she knew anything about this, and second, Jennifer should say she had actually seen Belinda and her father having lunch together. It would be just too bad if the business partnership broke up.

Jennifer had her meeting with Belinda's father. The friendship between the two families cooled, and before long, the partnership disintegrated. An embarrassed coldness settled in between Jennifer and her father, a coldness that has never quite thawed, not even after six years. Jennifer feels that she grew up then; she and her mother forged a deep woman-to-woman bond. They are best friends. Jennifer's mother forgave her father, though she was able to avoid admitting that she knew anything about it. Jennifer swears that she will *never* forgive him.

Both Sharon and Jennifer resorted to direct intervention in the Woman versus Woman conflict, even though neither of them dealt with the Other Woman. It is not a pretty situation for children or teenagers to be involved in. Neither of these cases resulted in divorce, and though both girls were profoundly affected by their experience, both feel that they were better off than if there had been a divorce. Both felt uncomfortable about their parents' sexuality, anyway, but believe they were more realistic about this than children of a previous generation would have been. Both saw the Other Woman as a threat to the family unit, and therefore to themselves.

Laura, aged 19, is one of those daughters who accepts her shipping magnate father's infidelities, and even goes on holiday with her father and one of a selection of his mistresses. If her mother knows about this, she gives no sign. Indeed, as things stand Laura 'covers' for her father; she is his chaperone. Her mother finds it easier to tell her friends that Hugo takes Laura with him on his business trips. The excuse is that Laura is 'learning the business'. Laura sees nothing wrong with either her or her father's behaviour – all his other women know that he'll never leave his wife. The family is not at risk, and her loyalty is not compromised. Her mother, an athletic former gym mistress, doesn't seem to know or to worry about it, so why should she? Laura and her mother have never got on, which probably goes a long way to explain her attitude.

Sometimes all the children in the family gang up against the Other Woman. It is important to stress here that we are not discussing a post-divorce situation.

Two days after their father left their mother for one of his colleagues at the biology laboratory, the three Clarke children decided to take matters into their own hands. Selma, the Other Woman, is convinced that the two younger boys, aged 14 and 12, were led by their sister, Felicity who was 15. They took Selma unawares in her office. Each one slapped her face once, in turn, and then fled from the building. Selma was not badly hurt, but the experience unnerved her. 'It was more than enough. I couldn't even think of having anything more to do with the father of such *monsters*. I got out. He went back to his wife. They were *his* children. He couldn't give them up.'

The academic background of the Clarke children – unusually intelligent and high achievers – is worth mentioning. Their maternal grandfather was a physician, and the grandmother lectured in English Literature. Their paternal grandparents were both violinists. Their mother was a physician, their father a biologist. As Selma admits, they were indeed a civilized, intellectual family. Fired by family loyalty the children went to war to defend their territory.

Selma cannot believe that the mother of the Clarke children was not the inspiration of their attack. The children's father was appalled that she could even think like that. It seemed clear to both that each was very different from what the other had thought.

Antonia's sons, 18, 15 and 9, were obliged to spend some weekends with their father Blair who was 53, in his small lovenest with his Other Woman, 25-year-old Mandy. None of them wanted to go; they hated sharing a small room next to the large room in which their father and Mandy slept. The eldest boy, Alan, was particularly resentful of Mandy's attempts to be 'buddies' with him. She used to encourage him to read more, to study harder for his A-Levels, as four years previously she had done. She had read history, too, and offered to help. Mandy, a slim and sexy girl, wandered about the flat shoeless and braless; she wore tight jeans and half-buttoned shirts and more than once Alan had seen her dash to the bathroom in a flimsy nightgown. The whole thing embarrassed him in every way. At first his mother used to try to joke about it, but that made Alan even angrier. After four such weekends Antonia astonished herself by saying, 'Why don't you tell your father she makes passes at you?'

'But she doesn't make passes at me!'

'So what? Tell your father Dougal saw her do it, too. Tell him he can ask Dougal, if he doesn't believe you. He won't, but just in case, we'll warn Dougal about what to say. Tell him you've got nothing against Mandy. It's not Mandy's fault, she's just that kind of girl, she can't help it.'

Alan did just this and, as his mother had predicted, his father did not ask Dougal about it. Blair was very understanding; he said he realized Alan felt uncomfortable and needn't spend every weekend with him. But the lovenest survived about six weeks after that, and then Mandy left. It was eight months before Blair moved back home, and then it was on the clear understanding that the Mandy incident would have to be treated as a 'closed chapter'.

That the affair would have disintegrated without Antonia's intervention seems highly likely. Antonia's tactic, however, is a fine example of the way in which the Woman versus Woman conflict is prosecuted. Antonia believes she acted on impulse when she made that suggestion to her son. But whether impulse or instinct, Antonia struck at Mandy's apparent strength – her sex appeal. By implying that its force was great enough to attract even his own 18-year-old son, the further implication was that it would also attract most young men. Blair, after all, was 53. This blow, aimed with laser-like precision, turned Mandy's greatest strength into her greatest weakness, she was like a grenade going off in her own hand.

Victory might have come anyway. Antonia's tactic brought it sooner.

The results of the deployment of children by mothers are not always so successful. Meg, 26, told her boys, aged 8 and 5, that if she had seen the bitch walking down the street with that nice new coat bought by *her* dad, when he lets his own kids go short, like the bitch in their father's life, she'd have pelted that bitch with hot chips, that's what *she* would have done. Which is precisely what the boys did. Which made matters worse.

The Woman versus Woman conflict is frequently a conflict of enraged desperation. When the humiliation of rejection is compounded by material hardship to her children, a mother's raw and primitive howl of fury can only be compared to the raw and primitive howl of childbirth itself. That her children went without, while their father's Other Woman wore a new summer coat, was a violation of Meg's maternity, to say nothing of her sense of natural justice. Meg's spite was an outlet, rather than an expression of fury, for the nature of it was such that it could never be expressed. Meg's behaviour was counterproductive, but to attribute that behaviour to nothing more than vindictive spite is to lose sight of a critical aspect of the Woman versus Woman conflict which is concerned with Meg's sense of natural justice. The summer coat worn by that other woman symbolized the virtual poverty that had been visited on Meg's children.

Alexander, a 32-year-old mathematics teacher, left his wife Beryl after twelve years and went to live with Sandy, aged 26, an unmarried mother with a child of 3. He also left his 10-year-old daughter Susan, a plump, laughing girl who had idolized him. Susan took to telephoning him from a call-box at school. 'Daddy, please come back to Mummy and me.' Then he would hear her sobbing and then the connection would be cut. This happened again and again for three weeks.

When Alexander visited her, Susan refused to see him. She

would rush to her bed and lie there with her eyes closed. She also refused to eat. She said she wasn't going to eat until her Daddy came home, and ate nothing for four days. Her mother begged Alexander to pretend to have returned, to come back for only a few days, to make believe that everything had returned to normal. She even said she'd talk to Sandy, if it would help; she said she would forgive Sandy everything if only she would agree to this. She would do anything Sandy asked, anything.

Alexander returned and watched his daughter's health improve, watched the colour return to her cheeks. When he decided to stay with his own family, Sandy said the whole thing had been a trick. Alexander didn't believe her, he told Beryl about it and they agreed only a *real* bitch could have even thought like that. . . . It is well known how often children implore their fathers to return to the family. Sometimes their mothers encourage them to do so, and sometimes the children do it of their own accord. Beryl insists that she had no part in Susan's behaviour. She admits, though, that when he agreed to pretend to have returned, she hoped he would stay.

If children are pawns of divorce, they are both the weapons and the target of the Woman versus Woman conflict. For the conflict continues after victory, even as it continues after divorce. The children are the targets and the weapons when the two women use them to get at each other. Maisie was 14 and her brother Thomas 12 when their parents divorced and their father Claude married Sabine, 24 and a fellow schoolteacher. Maisie's mother Angela was a lecturer in criminology. Staying access agreed by the courts meant that the children spent every other weekend with their father and Sabine. The flat, small to begin with, was made smaller by the many tropical plants which were Sabine's passion and which cluttered the living room in which the two children were compelled to sleep. One Sunday, when they were all in the car, and about to visit friends for Sunday lunch, Maisie said she had to go back to the flat; she had forgotten something important. Her father gave her the key, and she hastily uprooted several of Sabine's plants. She had told her mother she would do just that, her mother said she didn't blame her, but she'd better not tell her brother. When she returned home, her mother asked her if (as she put it) she'd 'carried out her mission.' When she said she had, her mother said, 'Good. Break a plate next time.'

Marjorie is resigned to feeling guilty for the rest of her life over having broken up her present husband's previous marriage. Her husband, Jack, feels guilty too. Marjorie is a 32-year-old solicitor who describes herself as an ardent feminist. Her husband Jack, aged 45, is marketing manager of a large international company. Jack and Marjorie met when her firm of solicitors was retained by his company. Marjorie is the sort of person who believes in candour, in being frank and forthright. She has decided never to have children; she cannot bear the thought that Jack 'might – just might' reject her children as he rejected those he already had.

They have been married for three years. Jack's daughter, Beatrice, was 11 when he left, and the two other children, Hugh and Saul, were 9 and 8. Marjorie says,

> 'It was not a bad marriage. It's just that Jack felt he couldn't communicate with anyone in that family. He says now that he probably would never have left if his daughter had been 14 then, and I agree with him.
>
> 'But the child resents me horribly, and I resent her too. I know it's irrational, but she reminds me of her mother. She doesn't even resemble her mother – she's much prettier – she takes after Jack. But she has all her mother's expressions, inquisitive eyes, critical lips, and the same high, bright voice. It's like having a whole gang of enemies, led by Beatrice, descending on me when they come to stay. I know they repeat everything to their mother, and I feel self-conscious *all* the time. I wouldn't dream of arguing in front of them, so when they leave I argue and then Jack

says, "Look, I didn't leave my wife to argue with you." And so I find myself saying things to them like, "I'll have to iron your shirts before we go out. I suppose your mother didn't have the time." Their mother's got all the time in the world. But I get sarcastic – their mother could and should go to work – she's a nurse – but she won't. At least if she worked, she could meet other people, create a life of her own. She wouldn't have the time to knit him socks and sweaters – he only wears them when the children come. But she sends him birthday cards and anniversary cards of the day she told him she was pregnant with Beatrice, their first meeting, of their marriage and so on. When she phones to speak to Jack, and I answer, she has the nerve to ask for *Mr Williams*. She tried sending cakes and biscuits with the children when they came, but I was firm about that, and I asked them not to bring any food if they wanted to come again. Jack couldn't understand this.

'Of course Louise's living standards have dropped, she had to sell the house and move to a flat, and Jack and I were more than fair about alimony and so on. We knew we were guilty. Or else I spend my own money on an extravagant dress for Beatrice, and then I ruin everything by saying "I'm trying to teach her to have some taste." But when she came to stay she would always wear her tatty clothes – not exactly patched, but she or her mother or both did their best to make her look like an orphan girl.

'So then I made the kids keep the clothes we bought for them in *our* flat, so she can't actually see them.

'When Louise found out about Jack and me, she phoned the receptionist, as well as my secretary, and told them all about me; told them she'd hate me for ever because I was taking her husband away. But I didn't – he left. I know how she feels about me – the same way I felt about her. I'm sure we each have fantasies about each other dying. Sometimes I even have fantasies about all her children dying, and then I hate myself even more than I hate her. It *is* depressing. If I were really honest, I'd come to terms with the fact that an important reason for my not wanting kids of my own is that I'm afraid of *her* feeling the same way about mine as I feel about hers.

'I don't think Jack's happy. I don't think I'm happy. I don't think either of us can face the thought of having done all this for nothing. Jack's a good father; I feel guilty about Jack, too. He knows that – he feels guilty about *me*. But we love each other. We must love each other. Why else would we stay married? *We've* no children . . .'

Marjorie consented to be interviewed because she thought the book was about second wives. She was at first hostile to the title *Woman versus Woman*, considered it reactionary as well as sexist. She was intrigued by the notion that Jack's wife's hysterical behaviour had made it all too easy for him to leave, and agreed that this could even have been a contributory factor to his decision to divorce. She said she wished she had heard of the Woman versus Woman conflict before; she felt she would probably not have given Jack up, but that she might have understood her own behaviour a bit better, and modified it somewhat. She said she'd spent more time thinking about Louise than about Jack: Louise had taken over her head, and she hated her because she'd felt she was stuck with her, and because she believed that Louise had turned her into a 'neurotic shrew'. She also agreed that a man seldom allowed an ex-husband to dominate his thinking in anything like the way a woman allows an ex-wife to dominate hers.

Ronnie, an only child, was 13 when his father, Ben, a heating engineer aged 40, left to set up house with 30-year-old Anita, a divorcée with two children, 4 and 6. Ronnie's mother, Barbara, a telex operator, aged 35, was adamant that Anita had ruined her life as she had ruined her son's life. But, as so often happens in this situation, she turned to her son for comfort. He became her confidant.

She would weep when she told him that his father was a

good man, a good family man who'd been led astray by a common tart, a wicked woman. She begged him not to speak to *her*, to refuse even to be in the same room as *her*, that no matter what the judge decided when the divorce came to court, he should say that he wanted to see his father, but not if it meant that he had to see *that woman*. 'And if they ask you if all this is what your mum wants you're to tell them I had nothing to do with it. Otherwise they'll make you go. And I don't know what they'll do to me.'

It had been a close relationship. Ben had been proud of his only son, his only child, who always tried so hard to please. Barbara had known she was on strong ground when she referred to Ben as a good family man. She had never said a bad word about his father. Instead she praised him, said he was the *best* husband, the *best* father.

Ronnie told his father he loved him and that whatever time he wanted him, he would get up at 6 a.m. and get on the train with his father when he went to work and then go home again, but he would never be in the same room as that woman – he'd rather go to prison. He said he was sorry, but he hated her enough to want to kill her. 'Beat me if you like, Dad,' he said, 'but I still won't go!'

'You won't see me then!' his father said.

And for three months neither Ronnie nor his mother saw Ben. Nor did they receive any support from him. It was hard, but they managed. She persuaded Ronnie to write to his father, twice a week, short letters about school, about how much he missed him. At his mother's suggestion Ronnie's notes, on about four or five occasions, referred to the past high moments of his young life; he mentioned the chemistry set his father had given him and how useful it still was; he said he'd watched *The Two Ronnies* on the telly and wished they could have been together; he hoped his father had enjoyed the last programme as much as he had; he thanked his dad for that lovely day they'd been to France on the ferry, and so on. Every letter mentioned how much he missed his father. The last letter contained one of those instant passport photographs 'in case you've forgotten what I look like, and so you'll see how I've grown, Dad.'

So far Ben had not replied to a single letter. However, only three days after he received that photograph he came home. Ronnie is now 14½ – those three months were not mentioned and, as Barbara says, if she has her own way they never will be.

Too often rejected wives poison their children's minds against their father. This Barbara did not do. She had never seen her husband as her adversary. But the Other Woman was her enemy and her son's enemy and she certainly poisoned her son's mind against that enemy.

Mothers who intrigue with their children as part of a strategy should not be confused with those mothers or fathers who poison their children's minds against their mother/father and stepparent. Parent-children alliances against the invader (Other Woman, or for that matter, Other Man) are not new. But the motives behind such alliances have been largely misunderstood, if not denigrated. While it has become fashionable to decree that parents should *not* stay together for the sake of the children, a silence surrounds those parents who do, and who know that this way there are fewer regrets.

Of course it is wrong to involve children in the Woman versus Woman conflict. One might well argue that the conflict itself is wrong, too. But it ought to be recognized that the members of a family that functioned well until the onslaught of ecstasy are obliged to defend themselves.

8

An aura instead of a status

The Other Woman is at least as much a victim of the fallacy that only a marriage that is weak or failing is susceptible to the Other Woman as the wife herself.

The assumption that no happily married man 'looks around' is one which implies that the mildest appreciative glance, the merest flirtatious twinkle – not to say chivalrous manner – only occurs in unhappily married men. Again and again the Other Women I spoke to used variations on the theme that 'he wouldn't have noticed me unless he was unhappy'; 'I couldn't have got into his life unless he was unhappy'; 'he wouldn't have asked me out unless he was unhappy'; and this whether he said so or not. In other words, he was not even required to say he was unhappy – *the unhappy state of his marriage was taken for granted*. A married man's approach, or invitation, is accordingly instant and obvious evidence that he is unhappily married. He is therefore entitled to look around. The new understanding that happiness is not a privilege but a right means that he has a duty to himself to find it. His marital status must somehow (magically) armour him against a constant bombardment of erotic stimuli. The smallest sign of mental fatigue signals discontent with what he has at home rather than appreciation of what the wider world has to offer. Now that sexual fulfilment has become as much of a social obligation as queueing –

even more obligatory, perhaps, than punctuality – prohibitions that might otherwise have disqualified someone's husband no longer apply. A husband is, after all, only exercising his right to pleasure which right exists by reason of his wife's default. 'She's not keeping him happy, she couldn't keep him happy, so why shouldn't I?' seems in the prevailing social climate a logical enough assumption. It needs to be stressed that the social revolution liberated men as much as women, since women were required to take responsibility for themselves; a married man's heart need no longer be troubled by any of those old-fashioned, inhibiting constraints. As Christopher Lasch says in *The Culture of Narcissism*, 'All women share in the burdens as well as the benefits of liberation, both of which can be summarized by saying that men no longer treat women as ladies.'

The effects of the women's liberation movement are still being felt even though the movement itself has mellowed. But both the sexual revolution and the women's movement resulted in social change. Couples live together before or instead of marriage and though the institution of marriage is not nearly as unpopular as the theory has it, living together has acquired a vague, paperless, acceptable status that will soon require a different sort of paper to formalize its 'extralegal' dimension.

The number of committed or uncommitted live-in-lovers has increased and society and parents have adapted to this as they have to so much else. (But to have your daughter live with an unmarried man is not quite the same as having her live with a married man.) Contraception has facilitated baby-proof relationships; marriage for some is an option, only to be taken up when the need to reproduce is founded on something stronger than mere biology. Technology has fostered a change in the biological aspects of pairing, but it has not so far invested a correspondingly applicable vocabulary for the unwed pair. Some sort of positive term is required, like 'contracé' for what was once a husband. Meanwhile our difficulty here is that the 'contracée' or, for us, the Other Woman is also known as the mistress, but for our purposes the Other Woman or mistress category refers to women who are in an intimate relationship with a married man.

One of the indications of how far the numbers of Other Women have increased is the fact that so many women and wives in this study mentioned their concern for daughters who were already entangled with a married man because of peer pressure, or had daughters whose friends had become the Other Woman. And more than one bewildered mother referred to the child her daughter intended to have by her married man. One of the consequences of this ever-increasing population of Other Women has been an increase not only in one-parent families, but, as one mother put it, in 'illicit grandparents' as well. It is a condition that has caused untold pain and misery to these women whose grandchild is also the child of their close friend's husband and even more pain when the birth of a child is still not enough of an inducement for the man to leave his wife. After all, that child is no longer his responsibility. For if women are now in charge of their own bodies, as they clearly are, that child or that consequence is hardly another woman's husband's responsibility.

The middle point between superiority and inferiority is said to be equality, and so it should be. Now men are not equal to women and women are not equal to men, and can never be; the trouble is that equality before the law, endorsed by statute, has still to be endorsed by technology, let alone nature. There are areas where absolute equality is absolutely viable (in child rearing, employment, pay, etc.) as there are areas where absolute equality is absolutely impossible (in cell structure, hormones, blood components). The difficulty is that notions of equality somehow get mixed up with notions of freedom. And the Other Woman is both a product and a victim of that freedom, and in the Free World, freedom and democracy are held to be indivisible. Sexual licence conveniently masquerades as sexual democracy.

Mistresses Anonymous was founded in the United States in 1976 by Melissa Sands.

'I was once a mistress, isolated, madly in love, and in distress. My personal trauma led to my organizing other mistresses in a group called Mistresses Anonymous, a group to share secrets and help each other. My Organization made me a national celebrity. Apparently there were more mistresses out there than I or anyone else had imagined.' (Melissa Sands, *The Second Wife Survival Manual*)

In 1982 the Other Woman's Forum was established in Washington, offering a counselling service and a nationwide newsletter. It was founded by two women who, like Melissa Sands, had suffered the anguish of being the Other Woman. Mid-week counselling sessions attracted very few women because they were 'staying at home waiting for their man to call. They were keeping themselves available for their men. Now we meet at the weekends. The men are with their wives and children then' (*The Standard*, August 1982).

Susan, 34, is one of the founders of the Other Woman's Forum. Her affair lasted two years; she left believing her married man would follow her and divorce his wife, but he did not leave his wife. Susan's remarks highlight the plight and the rise in numbers of Other Women.

'We believe that one in two women in America will at some time confront the possibility of an affair with an unavailable man, and we are telling them that they should feel no guilt. Look at the statistics – there are 5½ million more women than there are men in the States. Women are going to find a lot of men they want are already taken. Having an affair is merely a life situation.'

These two organizations arose out of a need; the fact that Other Women exist at all is an indication of their place in society, but, like alcoholics, they are neither condemned nor condoned.

The rise in the number of Other Women has been brought about by the sexual and contraceptive revolution, by the women's movement and by the increased divorce rate. But a significant cause of the increase in the Other Woman category, frequently overlooked, is the defeated wife, which is why it has become realistic to assume that almost every wife is capable of becoming the Other Woman. The initial interviewing for this study began in 1979, and during that time several defeated wives turned into Other Women, thus their experience gained on the other side of the Woman versus Woman conflict was put to maximum use. In some cases reluctance took less time to overcome than surprise.

Clearly, then, the Other Woman cannot be stereotyped, and in a world where morality is becoming more and more loosely defined, where the boundaries between right and wrong have lost clarity, the Other Woman cannot be said to be immoral: in many ways she is the product of her time, neither accepted nor condemned, yet branded placeless.

Some newly divorced women take themselves on the sexual merry-go-round hoping to restore their battered confidence. A real relationship is the last thing they consciously want. But the shock of ostracism, for those who find themselves suddenly excluded from the sort of social engagements that made up their lives, has triggered a defiance in the face of injustice, a revolutionary state of mind or attitude, which not only causes, but justifies, their placeless status as the Other Woman.

This revolutionary frame of mind is exemplified by Janet Smith, aged 45, a physiotherapist, mother of three teenagers, divorced for three years after twenty-two years of what she refers to as a 'fine marriage'. Janet would like to remarry, but has not yet met anyone with whom she feels she could form any sort of meaningful relationship, though she has had, she says, the 'odd adventure'. She is lonely, and considers the single life 'unnatural'. In common with most divorced women of over 40, she finds it difficult to meet 'unattached men'.

It was while she was having coffee with Margo, a colleague with whom she had recently become friendly, that her problem came up. Margo had had a similar experience to Janet, but was now remarried. She told Janet that if she wanted to find a new husband she was 'going to have to go out and find someone who was already married', which was, she admitted, exactly what she had done, because 'there are no unattached men out there.' She said, 'You just won't find one.'

Until then, Janet had not so much as considered the possibility of forming any sort of meaningful relationship with a married man. Though the 'odd adventures' referred to earlier had been with married men, she had not expected or even dreamed that 'anything serious' could develop. As it was, she'd felt badly about it.

Janet is a woman of average looks, not noticeably attractive, but not dowdy, with a neat figure and neat clothes and mildly religious. She thought about her colleague's advice very seriously, and conceded that it 'made sense'. Such a concession was, for Janet, revolutionary in itself. Janet had been adamant that she was 'not that sort of woman'. She was not the sort who looked at other women's husbands. There was a time when Margo's arguments would not have made any sort of sense to her at all. There was a time when she would have been appalled and horrified. But that time was long past. Now, far from horrified, Janet was grateful to her colleague for having spoken so frankly. Janet altered her approach to her 'odd adventures' and is now the Other Woman to a man who has been married for thirty-four years. Her life is 'less unbearable' than it had been.

Janet's reasoning is founded on pure pragmatism; she accepts that 'circumstances alter cases', and is certain that there was no alternative. She doesn't like what she is doing, and tries not to think about how the wife would feel if she knew, but feels no guilt. She's not sure whether the man would marry her if he were free, but thinks he 'might'. At any rate she would be happy to marry him, though she knows he has no wish to divorce.

Janet's thinking went against all her established standards. She had lived her life by the simple precept 'do unto others as you would have them do unto you.' She had known Simon, the married man in her life, and his wife Anne for about fifteen years. She and her former husband used to meet the Smiths quite regularly, and she and Anne were 'good acquaintances'. Since her divorce her social life had dwindled and she had seen them less frequently.

Like many a divorcée, Janet experienced not only her husband's rejection, but the rejection of many of her friends and acquaintances as well. She met Simon (by chance) outside their local supermarket and helped him carry his packages to the car. He invited her for a drink, and she accepted. Before that conversation with her colleague, Margo, she would not have offered to help him carry his packages.

One of Janet's postures in the Woman versus Woman conflict is to allow Simon to believe that she feels 'very bad' about his wife, a woman whom she 'rather likes' and admires. The truth is that Janet has *no* feeling for her. She is careful not to disparage her, and avoids saying anything directly against her. However, she *sympathizes* with Simon over his difficulties and differences with his wife, which is a way of showing him how important he is, not only to her but to the world at large. For example, when he told her how he and his wife had differed over how their 16-year-old daughter should be disciplined because she wasn't working hard enough at school, Janet's only concern was for *him*, and how hard this sort of thing was on *him*, etc. In other words, only Simon's feelings are relevant.

The triangle exists even when one of the three is ignorant of its existence, which means that even if Simon's wife has no idea about the relationship between her husband and Janet, she is one of those wives whom the Woman versus Woman conflict draws in anyway. Janet sees her as an adversary and treats her accordingly. She must somehow make Simon see that she is not only different from his wife, but better.

As more and more emphasis is placed on the need for emotional and financial independence, more and more wives retreat from all these unfortunates, like Janet, whose emotional and financial independence has been thrust upon them. The loneliness (which in many ways forced the Other Women into their placeless role) is thus intensified. If 'a woman divorced after 40 – after her childbearing years – is most likely to spend the rest of her life unmarried' (George Gilder, *Commentary*, November 1974), then it is equally likely that she will not remain celibate. Indeed, there are those who would say that she is one of the more honourable members of the Other Women brigade.

Articles in women's magazines, television programmes and films recognize this new category of Other Women and tend, increasingly, to cast her in the shape of a noble heroine. She is more and more seen as blameless – after all, that blame has been self-arrogated by the wife as well as allocated to her (as we discussed in Chapter 1). Numerous articles warn young women that married men break hearts, or instruct them on how to get that man away from his wife, or inform them how much they unknowingly contribute to shoring up his own marriage. These articles make little, if any, mention of his wife and children in their own right. Rather, the emphasis is on the difficulties or hardships the wife and children might inflict on the Other Woman. Contraception eliminates conscience as well as babies, and the Other Woman is not required to have either.

For many Other Women, the childless future is also the faceless future. Reproductive mechanisms age, and the number of Other Women who find themselves unexpectedly stricken by baby hunger is perhaps one of the saddest examples of how badly things have gone wrong. The half-childless marriage is but one of the consequences, and many second wives who claimed, and believed, that they did not want children of their own agreed to voluntary childlessness.

Enlightened experts of the mind seek to eliminate a central social ill such as guilt or, more specifically, a guilty conscience, so that those who take the conscious decision to become the Other Woman do so without the unnecessary complication of guilt. Irrational guilt has been taken to mean all guilt, just as neutrality has been taken to mean objectivity. This in turn has led to the prevailing wisdom that 'it's not my problem, it's your problem' which is very much a part of the rationale of many Other Women. Since the expression of sexuality has come to be taken as one of life's great quests and even greater achievements, for both men and women, in an attempt to redress the double standard, and in the much promoted belief that nothing is being taken from the wife, many women see the married man as desirable and often more desirable than the man who is not married.

There are, of course, many reasons for the desirability of the married man, and some young women who have never been married would rather go in for a relationship with a man who is not free than with one who is. It is this very lack of freedom that is so attractively compelling, if only because it facilitates the non-commitment that some women feel so desirable at a certain age and for a certain time. The idea of forbidden fruit is of little importance in its own right, though it does provide the extra sweetness of intrigue, mystery and sometimes even secrecy. It is perhaps worth mentioning that the secrecy that was once a *sine qua non* of the affair, and was as near a complete cloak as it was possible to be, is often only half a cloak, half a secret. For the younger Other Woman tells her friends, and may even introduce her married man to them, to show him off. She tells her friends what a great lover he is, and they tell him what she has told them, and he is even more flattered than he was at the beginning. It is perhaps not superfluous to add that her freedom gives her the ability to keep her options open, which means of course that there is a wider choice. But it is not the freedom to choose, but choice itself that must be limitlessly free, which is why married men should not be excluded. The right to limitless choice, then, is at one with the right to choose.

But besides freedom there are other, and equally important, perks. Married men are usually older than the Other Woman's male contemporaries, and therefore not only more practised but more grateful, and accordingly more ardent. The expectation of short hours of compressed intimacy, of compacted passion, sets their uncommitted love apart from and above the ordinary committed kind. And besides its regularity is infinitely preferable to those one-night stands whose love-making quality – like its disease potential – is perilously unpredictable. His superior age, a superiority that may be anything from five to forty years, means that he has far more money to spend than her contemporaries, and money, it has been said, is one of the most powerful artificial aphrodisiacs of them all.

Almost everyone has heard the wonderful story of the enraged wife who dumped her husband's dirty washing in his Other Woman's flat saying that if she wanted him, she'd better have his dirty washing too. Many Other Women make much of not having to wash his socks, it is a piquant symbol for the fact that while his socks belong to his wife, he belongs to her. If the washing of socks has never been noted for its ecstasy-inducing properties, not washing them adds to the delirium. It also keeps the mundane from the door. All the same, the fact that most married men have their socks, their shirts and so on attended to for them goes a long way toward the making of that attractive masculine appearance of strength and stability. Besides it adds immeasurably to that sexy aura of self-confidence. But some Other Women find something intensely pleasurable in the knowledge that the shirt he takes off and flings aside so carelessly, so easily, for her has been washed and ironed by his wife. Few Other Women are capable of feeling entirely indifferent towards a wife, however irrelevant she may be.

In *Having It all*, the influential Helen Gurley Brown said,

> 'I don't see how a single girl can survive *without* an occasional married man – to fill in the gaps, stave off hunger during lean days. . . . [The wife]. . . . What about her? I never worried about her. She's got a problem but you aren't *it*. *He* is it. A cheating husband will cheat with *somebody* – you are not that special. People always ask if this is my attitude – what would I think if *David* were cheating? Well, I would be *devastated*, but live by the sword, etc., etc. If someone can lure him from me, she's a good woman and I'll just have to deal with it. . . . I'm trying not to have that happen.'

It seems that any woman who may have scruples is strongly advised to shed them now. Apart from that, however, the implication in '*I'm trying not to let that happen*' is clear enough: a husband's 'cheating' is to be attributed to his wife. His cheating is her responsibility. But if that does happen, that is, if Mrs Brown's husband does cheat, will that mean that Mrs Brown did not try hard enough?

Let us consider for a moment Mrs Brown's advice that the Other Woman should not think of *herself* as the problem; the *man* is the problem. Let us accept for the sake of the argument that conscience has become as unnecessary and as cumbersome as an unwanted pregnancy. Conscience is an uptight hang-up only when it applies to individuals and not to groups. In the liberated society we are allowed, indeed encouraged to have a conscience about groups, the underprivileged, or the Third World, but on no account should this be applied to individuals. Staving off the hunger on lean days while letting an individual, such as a wife, starve has become an honourable enough pursuit. Because, Mrs Brown goes on, 'to me avoiding married men totally when you're single would be like passing up first aid in a Tijuana hospital when you're bleeding to death because you prefer an immaculate American hospital some unreachable distance across the border'. Better to let *her* bleed to death.

It is small wonder that the honouring of a quest for instant gratification has led to so little real gratification. The selfish (unfashionable word though it is), the self-involved self-love that self-styled gurus such as Mrs Brown advocates has become the goal of the individual. The only individual who counts is yourself, which is partly why (as noted earlier) the man at the centre of the Woman versus Woman conflict is so often irrelevant. (Has *he* become the sex object?) *Her* grief, *her* broken family is *her* problem. If he is the husband of your best friend, that, too, is *her* problem. After all, if someone as successful and, at 59, as experienced as Mrs Brown, says, 'I never worried about her', why should a younger woman of, say, 19, worry about her either? Most young women of 19 believe that a 59-year-old public and successful figure must be wise as well as experienced.

It was to 'fill in the gaps, stave off hunger during lean days' that led Mabel to turn to Ralph, her brother-in-law. Ralph was married to Mabel's sister, Elaine, younger by two years. Ralph and Elaine had been married for four years. Mabel's husband was an NCO posted abroad, and it was when Ralph, an electrician, went to help her with some household chores that Mabel, wearing fishnet tights, confided how much she missed the physical side of her marriage. Ralph offered to help out at once. They made love instantly. He found that Mabel was as outrageous in her bed as in her dress. She was altogether more adventurous than her younger sister. Indeed, her sexual behaviour with Ralph was extraordinary enough to cause her to worry that she was 'unnatural'. She enjoyed the sort of sex that her sister permitted only reluctantly. Ralph and Mabel agreed that things would have been different if Elaine had not been so inhibited. Elaine was, in a way, responsible for the way things turned out. The emergency help Ralph gave during that 'lean time' became more permanent.

Elaine withdrew from the Woman versus Woman conflict and surrendered unconditionally because she didn't want to win. Nor does she 'particularly want to live'. She speaks of suicide. She and her sister had shared a flat before their marriages. They had been close, they had been real friends. They hate one another now, but Elaine cannot bring herself to tell Mabel's husband what has happened. She is afraid of a double murder.

9

Wheeling and dealing

An offer of marriage is felt by many women to be crucial proof of a man's real feelings. Even those Other Women who have an intellectual understanding of why their married men cannot offer marriage can't help *feeling* that if he 'really loved her' he would. It is a feeling that her parents and her friends take great pains to reinforce. Resignation never quite eliminates that nagging, clinging doubt that if only she meant enough to him, he would divorce his wife *for* her. Meanwhile, even if only in name, his wife has what ought to be hers. She feels she has more right to him than his wife. Though the offer of marriage is not as important to those who have no wish to marry their married men, it is nevertheless perceived to be a significant measurement of the strength of the man's involvement. As the Other Woman's need to be married grows, it is all too easy for her to perceive the wife (and not the patriarchal system) as her real enemy.

Eventually, though still not entirely convinced, the Other Woman becomes convinced *enough* to believe that it is the wife and children, and nothing but the wife and children, who stand between her and her happiness. And this also applies to those to whom it was made clear from the very beginning that divorce was unthinkable. It is less hurtful to believe that 'if he could, he would, but he can't' than 'he wouldn't even if he could'. Therefore, despite all evidence to the contrary, many Other Women persist in believing that 'he would if he could but he can't'. That he can't is entirely due to one or a combination of the following: the spite, greed, jealousy, blackmail (emotional and other), and neurosis of that lucky bitch who is his wife. It is the sort of rationalization that successfully exonerates both herself and her married man.

The wife, then, is the stumbling block, the obstacle that stands in her way. The wife fences her out. Some, helped by feelings of destiny and resignation, manage to have no feelings for the wife. It is, after all, easier to live with indifference than with hate. But for many *she is hated because she is there*, and many wives, hoping to appeal to the Other Woman for the sympathy they are sure she must feel, are shocked when they find hatred instead. The unexpectedness of the hatred leaves many wives bewildered, shocked, and wounded to the point of derangement. For her part, the Other Woman is confounded too. How, she wonders, can she be expected to have any sympathy for the woman who has him? Why, she asks herself, should she cede to the married woman's wishes? What has the married woman ever done for her? Although the single woman may never have suffered at the hands of the married woman she wants to replace, she has probably suffered enough already from other wives' envy, fear, pity and scorn. Why should she be loyal to married women *ever*?

The Other Woman has the power, as the wife sees it, to make her family whole again. All the Other Woman need do is 'give him up, not for me, but for the sake of his innocent children'. It should not be thought that this appeal is never answered or respected. Sometimes it makes the Other Woman 'realize what she is doing'; it brings her 'down to earth', and she withdraws. Often the husband who has lost the 'only real love' of his life does not go in search of another, but stays with his wife, and sometimes the quality of the marriage is improved.

Sometimes the physical presence of the wife as a human

being, and not merely as a concrete obstacle, is enough to provoke sympathy for her. This may well lead to an appreciation of her own role in the potential overall suffering of the family. And then, again, a chance meeting with the wife has led many an Other Woman to discover that she actually likes the wife more than she likes the husband. Realizing that in the mind of the Other Woman she is no more than a vague and unreal notion, some wives arrange a chance meeting with her. It is possible for the Other Woman to end the conflict by giving up her married man; to relinquish a conquered target is a way of consolidating victory.

Maureen was married for the first time when she was 30 years old. Up until then she had several affairs with married men, but as soon as she met their wives she ended the affair. She could not continue with the relationship when she saw the wife as a 'real person', and not as 'some shadowy figure somewhere in his life'.

Referring back to this period of her life before marriage Maureen said, 'when you are single, everyone is fair game. You are attracted to men who may, or may not, be married'. She has been involved on three different occasions with a married man, and as soon as she saw that the wife was a 'normal person like you or me', she found that the affair 'became impossible'. It seems that for many Other Women the wife is only a figment in her own imagination, or an 'old hag who goes around in bedroom slippers'.

The two examples cited below indicate the way in which a wife is seen as a problem, rather than a person. The problem is as real, and as impersonal, as, say, inflation.

When the Other Woman is young and inexperienced her apprehension of the realities of the situation is bound to be limited. Anne, aged 21, and Mark, aged 45, fell 'passionately in love'. Anne thought that Jean would not 'mind' about the divorce 'too much' because she was already 45 and probably 'cared more about her grandchildren than about him'. Needless to say, Anne had a doting grandmother – children seldom see their parents as sexual beings and Anne thought

Mark's wife 'wasn't interested in sex and that'. Mark 'talked about his kids', two daughters aged 19 and 17, and Anne, curious because they were 'nearly the same age' as herself, asked if she could see what they looked like. It turned out that Mark always carried their photographs in his wallet. One of the photographs came as a profound shock to Anne. It showed three women, one of whom was his wife. Anne saw with her 'own eyes' how young and pretty his wife looked, 'even though she was old'. The photograph made her 'feel bad', made her feel 'different about Mark'. She found she 'couldn't go on with it' and waited for about two weeks after that (because she 'didn't like to hurt him') to give him up.

Betty was 27 and a mother of four when she fell in love with Peter, who was 43. Her own marriage was not happy, and she and Peter had much more in common with one another than she and her husband. Peter had been married for twenty years to June, a 'very cold lady'. Betty and Peter felt at once that they were made for each other, and they were so sure of this that 'we felt we'd been reborn'. Though still careful to keep the affair a secret, two divorces were being contemplated.

It was decided that Betty should see a solicitor, and Peter made the appointment for her. The solicitor began by saying, 'So you don't want your own husband.' 'No.' '*So you want someone else's husband.*' This brief, bald statement suddenly brought home the reality that Peter was, in fact, someone else's husband. Betty had known that Peter was married, but *she had seen him as a man, and not as a husband*, let alone someone else's husband. The incontrovertible fact that he was also a husband had eluded her. Reality was compounded still further when the solicitor added that it was very difficult to 'build your happiness on someone else's unhappiness'. As so often happens, Peter had shared her preoccupation and anxiety with what would happen to *her* children and how *her* own husband would 'take it'. Betty had reckoned with only one husband, her own husband. That Peter was a husband ought to have been a self-evident and omnipresent reality. And yet it is not altogether strange that this harshly central reality escaped Betty's attention. That passion heightens some realities even as it eliminates others is one of its glories. Betty ended the affair, and six years later is still married. Peter and his wife did not divorce either. She has not seen Peter since then, has not even 'bumped into him'. She 'thinks of him all the time', he will be an 'important part of her life forever', he is 'one of those things that you can learn to live with, and to accept'.

Both Anne and Betty had taken victory for granted. For them, the wife had had no chance, and so they believed they had not been involved in any sort of Woman versus Woman conflict at all. Anne (who saw the wife only in terms of a grandmother) had no idea whether or not the wife knew anything about her. Betty now thinks that Peter's wife must have known. Peter had once told her that he had 'touched his wife's tummy, and she had responded at once.' At the time, Betty had taken it for granted, as she had taken her victory for granted, that the sex had gone from Peter's marriage. It would seem that if there was no Woman versus Woman conflict for Betty, the same was not true of Peter's wife. Passion obliterates reality, and in the heat of the moment responsibilities are forgotten. Its inordinate power to erase reality, however briefly, is one of the main motors of all love affairs, which is especially true, perhaps, of extramarital love affairs. Though some realities are obliterated others are illuminated. Very often wives fall among those realities subsumed by passion. She is only one of the many externals that are irrelevant to those compressed bonds of infinity that are the stuff of which committed infidelity is made.

Rather than hate the man in the middle the two women engaged in the Woman versus Woman conflict will hate each other. This does not mean that the man in the middle always escapes hatred and enmity – far from it. It goes without saying that wives and Other Women direct and vent their fury on the man as well.

If hatred is a by-product of jealousy, rejection is its

consummation. Many wives whose husbands are involved with the Other Woman would rather not hear a word against their husbands, and frequently defend them from criticism. But any remarks and observations that can be directed against the Other Woman and her motivations will be both gratifying and comforting. When asked how they felt about the wife, or about the Other Woman, almost all of those women who were engaged in the Woman versus Woman conflict responded thus: *I hate her. I hate her.*

A case in point is Adele, 38, married for nineteen years to Douglas, who is 42 and a data processing manager. A full-time housewife and mother of three, Adele was utterly devastated when she discovered that her husband was engaged in a serious affair. It was while the identity of the Other Woman was still unknown to her that she turned to her friend Janet for advice and support. She considered Janet, an attractive, lively woman in her early fifties, to be 'wise in the ways of the world'. When she confided in Janet she had not yet communicated anything of what she knew to her husband. Janet advised her to continue with this tactic. Indeed, four months were to pass before Adele was forced to admit to her husband that she knew about his Other Woman. Adele believes her marriage withstood the affair largely because she followed Janet's guidance and counselling. However, Adele still recalls her amazed and horrified reaction to one of Janet's casual remarks against her husband, Douglas. The strain of keeping her knowledge of his affair a secret from her husband had begun to take its toll. A slim woman to begin with, Adele lost about a stone in weight, and insomnia was etched into her expression and around the eyes. She knew she looked haunted and tortured, and like so many wives engaged in the conflict never quite succeeded in overcoming what she described as 'that grim hang-dog look'. It was because she looked ill and tired that her friend remarked how much she would like to 'wipe the floor with Douglas' because of what he was doing to Adele. Adele's immediate instinct was to defend Douglas, and then to seek reassurance from Janet that she would never breathe a word of any of this to him.

For a long while after this Adele felt that she and her friend were not on the same wavelength after all. Because how could Janet blame Douglas when, according to Adele's way of thinking, Douglas had almost nothing to do with what was happening? All that was the work of the Other Woman. All her hatred (and she said she had plenty of it) went to the Other Woman; none of it went to Douglas.

Looking back, years later, Adele believes that the strength of her need to protect Douglas from the Other Woman overwhelmed all other considerations. She has never blamed him; instead, she has convinced herself that he was pursued. He was however a naive and immature man, and she is certain he will not be so easily fooled again.

Maggie, 32, a receptionist, married for two years after having lived with Jim, a plasterer, for eight years, is one of those wives who did not hate the Other Woman because she was 'beneath contempt' and an 'obvious tart'. They had no children and were an unusually happily married couple. Deeply religious, they took eight years to arrive at their decision to marry. Both were determined to honour their vows. The Other Woman in the story was a waitress called Nora. Maggie heard about it from a wellwisher, the wife of one of Jim's workmates. When Maggie confronted him with what she knew he did not deny it, nor would he offer to give Nora up. He admitted he had thought of leaving Maggie, and continued to see Nora for about four weeks.

Maggie was in tears most of the time, and after about three weeks of weeping and sobbing recriminations, found that she could not go to work. She had begged Jim to stay at home one Monday night, had sunk to her knees, and, sobbing hysterically, collapsed in a heap on the floor. Jim left her there, lying on the floor like a bundle of dirty washing, and did not return until the following night. Maggie was simply unable to move from where he had left her, which was where Jim found her when he came home to change after work the next day.

Maggie's strange behaviour shocked him. She was silent and withdrawn; she stayed at home and didn't even go to the shops. Jim had to get the food in. Maggie would cook for him, but could not eat. Jim saw Nora three more times and then broke the whole thing off.

They made it up, and made love, but Maggie could not forgive him. Eleven months have passed, and still she cannot forgive or forget. She felt there was nothing left to build on. Jim was not the man she had thought he was, and all his faults on which, as she puts it, she had smiled, were brought into intolerable relief. She could not forgive him, and he knew this. One day, she decided that the only way she could have some peace would be to kill him. She told her father she wanted a really sharp freezer knife, and asked him to get one for her. When he gave it to her, he warned her to keep it in its sheath, because it could easily kill a person. She took the knife and hid it away.

She was obsessed with Jim's betrayal. Jim had ruined their marriage, ruined their lives. She went over and over this in the privacy of her mind, and with Jim, who admitted that he'd been weak and who begged for forgiveness. One night she tried to strangle him, and though his neck was black and ugly with bruises the next day, he forgave her, and said he knew she wouldn't really be able, or even want to be able to kill him, which was why he hadn't even really defended himself.

Maggie says it was not her jealousy of the Other Woman that tormented her. It was the unshakable knowledge that Jim had actually thought of leaving her that unnerved her so. She translated disappointment into rage, and was engulfed. The rage crawled over her skin and itched, it grabbed her insides, but there was always more to be devoured. She longed for peace, and again thought of killing him. One night, in an uncontrollable but icy inner rage, as he lay asleep in bed, she went to the kitchen to fetch the freezer knife, but had forgotten where she had hidden it. She took another knife and marched into the bedroom and really meant to kill him. Jim heard her and awoke. He saw both her and the knife in time, and moved, and the knife pierced his shoulder instead of his chest. And again, he forgave her and begged her for forgiveness.

Maggie has now arrived at some sort of understanding of Jim's ecstasy. She concedes that Jim had no more control over his ecstasy than she had over her rage. He had not wanted to leave her any more than she had wanted to kill him. He was a casualty of her need for peace, a need so great that its achievement would have been an ecstasy of a sort. Jim was a casualty of that potential ecstasy, just as she had been a casualty of his ecstasy.

Maggie was one of those women to whom the handling of victory did not come easily.

Maggie's attitude is exceptional. The stunning frequency with which the two women express unequivocal hatred for one another warrants special attention. It might therefore be helpful to discuss the shape and form of the vengeance that followed in its wake.

It seems the plotting of revenge against the Other Woman offers a certain consolation, a safer peace than the kind contemplated by Maggie. The fantasy of 'getting even' is at the same time the hope that a redistribution of suffering will somehow equalize it: if I hurt her then I will hurt less. Vengeful acts, however, should be seen in the context of despair rather than spite.

Now 31, and once again involved with a married man, Gemma, a fashion designer whose beauty and style is of the crowd-stirring kind, spent two and a half years trying to get Jake (the first married man with whom she was involved) to leave Cindy, his wife. Cindy travelled a great deal and would be away for three months at a stretch. Their small son would be sent to his grandparents, and Gemma and Jake lived in his and Cindy's flat. 'Terribly in love', convinced that 'she'd found Mr Right', Gemma found 'piffling details like his marriage and child very irrelevant'. Of course, when she lived in Jake and Cindy's flat she examined all of Cindy's things, and one day destroyed all Cindy's and Jake's wedding photographs. Unable to stop herself, Gemma had taken scissors and systematically snipped the photographs and the negatives until she had reduced them to confetti.

Throughout their eight-year affair Maude had never been allowed to spend an entire night with Fred, but she was on intimate terms with the house in which he lived with his wife, June. She and Fred spent whole days there while June was at work. Towards the end of the affair she found herself slashing June's diaphragm.

At 38, Sally is an attractive, warm and motherly woman. She is the kind of person other people turn to in emergencies. She avoids being officious, yet her practicality calms others. During the early years of marriage and maternity, Sally ran a playschool co-operative from her home. This way she was able to take care of her three children and supplement the family income at the same time. When the children grew older, Sally joined an advertising agency and is now one of their senior executives. Twelve years ago, when she had been married for six years, Sally began an affair with Rex, an economist. In all those twelve years they have had only six weekends together. Sally, however, has spent whole days in Emma's home. Sometimes she wore Emma's nightgowns. Once Rex's son, aged 11, came home from school unexpectedly and found Sally and Rex in bed together. That night he told his father: 'I can blackmail you now, Dad.' Sally has not been able to determine whether or not Emma knows what is going on.

Cynthia and her daughter Natalie plotted a joint revenge. This was understandable enough; Gloria, 23, had been Natalie's best friend and was now her father's Other Woman. She and her mother went to Gloria's flat and waited for her; they had no difficulty gaining access as one of Gloria's room-mates knew Natalie well enough to let her in before she went out. Gloria had no sooner arrived than the mother held her down while her daughter cut off her hair. Gloria's copper tresses reached below her waist; she used to spend hours ironing them. Her hair was all she had; it made her almost beautiful, though she was otherwise plump and awkward. Whether Cynthia's husband found Gloria without her hair no longer attractive, or whether his wife's altogether uncharacteristic action moved him to a greater respect of her remains a mystery. He merely told his wife and daughter that he would not be seeing Gloria again.

Andrea knew that after lunching with her one Saturday afternoon, her best friend Iris would be trysting with her husband at Iris's flat. (Iris's husband was away.) She served steak and salad – her French dressing was more than ordinarily spicy. It had been necessary to disguise the liquid paraffin she had used instead of oil. The afternoon, she was sure, was ruined. The symptoms began even before Iris left. Such consequences as there were are unknown to Andrea. She never asked, but the friendship cooled. That ploy was a source of endless amusement to Andrea – she felt better about the whole thing, and her mood lifted enough to become more like the woman her husband had known before she had found out about his affair with her friend.

Even two years after Sarah's affair with Adam had ended she found herself giving way to a vengeful impulse. She had visited some friends who lived in the flat over Adam and his wife. It was in the early hours of the morning that she saw Adam's wife's bicycle standing in the hall. She slashed the tyres and then felt shame instead of exhilaration.

Ethel hated Fred's wife, Rosa. She hated her even more when Fred went away without her. She arranged for Rosa to be woken up by an alarm call, and telephoned her through the night.

The telephone is, of course, a convenient weapon of revenge. Bernice and Philip were constantly plagued by the telephone after he left his wife, Isabel. And yet they could not prove that it was Isabel who was making the calls. Whoever it was telephoned from a call-box. In the end Bernice decided to have Isobel followed by private detectives. It proved to have been a good investment.

It is extraordinary how often the Other Woman, once the affair is over, finds it necessary to tell the wife all about it.

Up until the moment that Hilda appeared in Mary's office, Mary had no idea either of Hilda's existence or of the fact that an Other Woman had entered her husband's life five months previously. Hilda sat down and said she had something private to tell her. Mary insisted that she didn't believe her, whereupon Hilda began with deadly accuracy to describe Mary's flat. She told her of the paintings on her walls, of the contents of her wardrobe. She had been there on at least eight occasions. What saved Mary was Hilda's triumphant expression. She enjoyed hurting her, she enjoyed this so much that Mary took her turn at doing the same thing. She told Hilda that she was at least the eighth woman she knew about – there were scores and scores whom she'd never met. Mary vowed to herself that she would say nothing to her husband; she would not, as she put it, take the bait.

Sheila mailed Henry's underpants to his wife. Frances sent, by recorded delivery, all of Gavin's love letters and their envelopes to his wife. Wives sent letters too. Cicily and her husband Oliver were stationed in Germany where he was an officer. Once when he was ill she fetched his mail for him. She recognized the handwriting on one of the envelopes as belonging to a close friend, Pearl. She steamed open Pearl's letter, and then did the same to the other letter. It seemed Oliver had made two assignations for the two consecutive weekends that he expected to be on home leave in England. Cicily merely placed the letters in new envelopes, but reversed the order of the assignations. Each woman received the letter the other had sent. Cicily added a postscript informing both of them that Oliver's comments about their sex life had not been at all accurate. Not even flu could stop him. He was at it all the time.

One of the most devastating and exciting, as well as most

frequent, of all the many forms of vengeance is that of the ex-wife who seduces her former husband. Those wives who practised this reported sensations of satisfaction and achievement on several levels. For one thing, the sex was better than.it had ever been: so good that fairly long-standing affairs developed, and in four cases a remarriage.

Dawn was one of those wives who by her own admission engaged in that activity with the sole purpose of reporting back to her successor.

Dawn's children were quite small, 8 and 6, when Barney left her after a ten-year marriage for her cousin, Sybil. Dawn said,

> 'I burned, but it was a slow burn. It went on for about three years. I swore I would get my own back. She never lets him out of her sight. She's always with him when he comes for the kids. So when Barney came to pick them up on the Saturday afternoon, I knew he'd have to be on his own, because she'd just given birth. I sent a bouquet of red roses to myself – the girl at the florist addressed the envelope – and when they were delivered I called out to the man to leave them outside the front door. I knew he'd look at the card, even try to open it. When he arrived I answered the door wearing nothing but a bath towel and perfume. He was holding the bouquet. I pretended I thought he'd brought them.
>
> 'Well, he came in, I invited him because of the flowers, I said. I told him the kids were out – had thought he wouldn't be allowed to come *alone*. He looked sheepish, and we sat down, and I brought him a beer, and then before you knew it, we were making love. I knew him well in that area, you see. So, just while he was coming (he goes mad when he comes!) I ripped his back, hard, cut the skin, slashed it! And, of course, he couldn't stop me. He was furious. I was afraid he'd kill me! He called me every name you can think of, and ran for his life.
>
> 'The next morning I went to see her – *before* official

visiting hours. I said I'd come from Edinburgh especially to see my first cousin, Sybil. So they let me in. She almost died when she saw me walk in with that bouquet. I simply told her what Barney had done – and she could look at his back if she didn't believe me. It was worth it. I got her out of my system.'

But perhaps one of the most amusing accounts of vengeful behaviour is to be found in a newspaper story recounted by Wendy James and Susan Jane Kedgley in their book *The Mistress*.

'In Vienna a woman found pictures of another woman in her husband's wallet. Recognizing the nude girl as her supposed best friend, she had each of the photographs blown up to poster size and pasted them up around the city with captions like "Behold the adulteress" and "Lock up your husband when you see this woman." She ended up in court on a charge of displaying obscene photographs and was given a token five days' imprisonment. When she came out of prison she was reconciled with her husband.'

The Woman versus Woman conflict seems to call forth gutter feelings from *all* women, even those who would normally be considered 'ladies'. Indeed, one would be doing the women discussed earlier a terrible injustice if one said they were not ladies. The Man versus Man brings out gutter feelings, too, but these are usually resolved in a direct physical confrontation, or drunken bouts. Any understanding of the Woman versus Woman conflict requires an understanding of the difference between men and women. However displeasing it may be to acknowledge this, one is hard put to imagine a man cutting up the clothes of his rival or leaving his underpants in his rival's house. It may be that because women (on the whole) do not have a man's brute strength, they have been compelled to resort to this kind of battle posture. Of course *some* women physically attack their rivals. There is no doubt that women have a subconscious awareness that their physical desirability has a shorter lifespan than a man's. And women, through the traditional acceptance of male promiscuity, have traditionally suffered more than men. As a result perhaps the sense of betrayal by one of their own kind triggers off some as yet unidentified biological reaction that propels them, in spite of themselves, towards a brand of savagery that would bewilder most men. But if the causes of what appears to be essentially female behaviour could be established, there would be a far more realistic understanding of the relationship between the sexes. For it would seem that in their sexual relationships men and women relate to one another in terms of the sum of their differences, rather than in terms of their similarities. It is, after all, the sexuality factor that sparks off the Woman versus Woman conflict in the first place. Whatever else the sexual act is, it is also primitive. A celebration of the primitive, perhaps, but primitive none the less.

The cutting up of a rival's clothes is far more profound than a simple act of spite. But it is only when it is understood why it is significantly more rare for men not to behave like this than it is for women that the necessary societal adjustments can even begin to be made.

10

Not so much naked as skinless: the best friend betrayal

A striking number of Other Women are close friends of the wife, and almost everyone has heard, at least once, of the husband who ran away with 'his wife's best friend'. The Other Woman who is 'best friends' with the wife is enough of a commonplace to have become a cliché. Very often the Other Woman is, if not one of the wife's close friends, one of her acquaintances. Of course, the Other Man 'takes away' his best friend's wife, too, but close friendships between men rarely achieve anything like the complex intensity of a friendship between two women. As Gail Sheeny says in *Pathfinders*, 'Women find it easier to build friendships – by which is meant genuine, loyal, non-competitive relationships – with other women than men do with other men. Friendships among men are rather rare, except, significantly, among the high well-being men.'

True, young men of today are re-ordering their priorities, and many of them are attaching more and more importance to emotional matters.

One of the reasons why men do not form close friendships may be that work has always been more important, and perhaps more comfortable than intimate relationships of a non-sexual nature. In *The Seasons of a Man's Life*, the author states:

> As a tentative generalization we would say that a close friendship with a man or woman is rarely experienced by American men. . . . The distinction between friend and acquaintance is often blurred. . . . We need to understand why friendship is so rare, and what consequence this has for adult life. . . .

A further reason may be that most men have long believed that emotions and their analysis belong more properly to women than to men.

This is not to say that men are without emotion, rather that they have allocated the understanding and the interest in it to women. For one thing, men were not supposed to feel enough to make them weep, and for another, emotion of that sort was regarded as 'womanish'. Men were supposed to be alien to the world of emotion, though not to the world of passion. At any rate it is fair to say that the components of a friendship between two men are vastly different from those between two women. By and large, other than to a minister or a doctor, men have looked to women for their emotional support, sustenance and comfort – men gave shelter and women gave comfort.

Most women need other women friends. Friendships between women are made up of intricate layers of intimate details. Nurturing has long been part of the female role and women turn to other women for emotional comfort, support and understanding. For most women, the emotional as well as the physical wellbeing of their families is a prime concern, and this is as applicable to those women who combine two careers as it is to those who only work at home.

Friendship plays a significant role in the Other Woman syndrome. Large numbers of displaced wives claim that they were displaced by a friend of one sort or another. Many wives seem to believe that the Other Woman who was once a friend is not only frequent but usual, and this applies to as many of those wives who had faced the Other Woman as of those who had not.

For the best friend, many of the uncertainties that are common to most courtships are eliminated. When, as so often happens, sexual boredom sparks an unusual sexual awareness in a potential partner who is new, though not strange, the easy familiarity between the husband and his wife's friend means that a certain intimacy has already been established. Long before their sexual connection, they are trusted friends. Their subterranean or informal courtship, then, is founded on mutual trust as well as chemistry. Their sexual connection is an extension of friendship and trust. It is this friendship and trust that makes the sexual connection not only more instantaneously important but far safer than the sort of casual sex that is also, and often, the result of sexual boredom. But when the two protagonists are close friends the shape and the consequence of the Woman versus Woman conflict is greatly altered. The Other Woman who is also the wife's best friend will wage a very different campaign from the Other Woman who has never met the wife. That the wife is unaware of her best friend's intentions does not mean that war has not been declared, but rather that the Other Woman is, in Nathan Bedford Foster's famous phrase, 'the fastest with the mostest'. The best friend connection therefore warrants examination.

One of the explanations for the frequency of the best friend as Other Woman is that it is so easy to allow a family intimacy to develop into what has become known as a 'one-to-one relationship'. The best friend finds that she is on safe and familiar territory, her frequent presence requires little or no explanation, and what is more, she is always welcome. Her easy access to the family means that she is able to make her own observations and draw her own conclusions. Of course she has extra private information as well. Few husbands are aware how many details of their private behaviour are exposed to, and examined by, their wife's best friend. But her trusted status is, of course, her most powerful weapon, if only because she is above any and all suspicion. (It may not be superfluous to add here that a wife who is suspicious of her own best friend can so easily be dismissed by both her husband and her best friend as being psychotic, mad or deranged. And in these instances, many wives grow, or are persuaded, to fear that they are indeed paranoid, as Chapter I has shown.)

Certainly the best friend believes herself to be on safe ground because of her in-depth knowledge of what she would be getting into – not for her the dangers of the unknown. She is well acquainted with his faults, to which (as she tells herself) his wife 'overreacts' in any case. If she is married and has children of her own, she knows what sort of a father he is, and if she has not yet had any children, she is able to predict, on the face of the evidence, what sort of father he will be to her unborn children. This last, however, is often the reason for the break-up of the new relationship; the Other Woman realizes that her future children might also be abandoned.

Sometimes the married man represents a challenge solely because the Other Woman sees his wife as a truly worthy rival, and so the real target then is not the man, but his wife. However, it may happen that when he gives up his wife he loses some of his magnetism, which is why some Other Women sour, and send the man back home again. There are many kinds of truly worthy rivals. The wife may be a woman of unusual distinction, say, a famous actress, startlingly beautiful or stunningly successful. Or she may have that distinction given to so many ordinary women, the distinction of being a close friend, or even a relation. In these cases it is difficult to discern how it can be said that the Other Woman is not involved in a direct act of aggression against the wife.

The motivations for choosing the husband of a friend as a lover are as complex as they are varied.

Audrey and Francine, who we met in Chapter 1, were best friends from the age of 10. Childhood best friends are but one of the variations of the best friend relationship. Close friendships begun only in adult life can take on the qualities of the best friend relationship. Since their friendship broke up, Audrey has held endless post-mortems on that friendship. The defection of her husband to her best friend was, needless to say, a double betrayal. All the same, Audrey felt that 'after having lost a husband what you want to do more than anything is to cry on your best friend's shoulder. Since your best friend knows all about you and your husband, you needn't feel disloyal to him. . . .' The knowledge that one has lost not only one's husband but one's best friend as well implies a double rejection.

The ongoing autopsy on the nature of their friendship has led Audrey to conclude that 'taking Eddie away' was one way of getting even with her. She had not realized that Francine had been in competition with her, even though it had been fairly obvious to everyone that she was much prettier than Francine. Painfully thin, with a leathery skin and a pocked and sallow complexion, Francine must have felt markedly inferior to her best friend. Audrey had a curvaceous figure, rosy cheeks and a pure unblemished complexion. Audrey was the sort of person who got along with everyone, whereas Francine was shy and somewhat diffident in her relationships with others. Audrey was an extrovert, while Francine was an introvert, and Audrey had felt that they complemented each other perfectly. Audrey now believes that because her own superiority was unquestioned, she took it for granted. Francine understandably never did, so she got even. Francine apparently liked and admired whatever Audrey liked and admired. Audrey always helped her choose her clothes, furnishings, etc., and she often bought a thing just because Audrey had one. Francine always wanted what Audrey had, and this included Audrey's husband. Whether or not some degree of subconscious rivalry is common to all friendships, Audrey now believes that Francine must have always looked upon her as a rival.

However, 'Best Friends since Childhood' is but one of the

variations of the best friend connection. One of the consequences of the technological revolution has been occupational mobility. The Global Village has meant that jobs are relocated, not only in different towns, but in different countries, and even hemispheres. This has in turn meant that the best friends relationship is formed with all the urgency that goes with travel. Families newly arrived in strange towns or countries need to belong to some sort of group. To a family posted abroad, the ex-patriate community is at least familiar in terms of language, custom and so on.

Uprooting a family is an emergency of a sort, and indeed, even moving house in the same street is a traumatic event. Occupational mobility leads to the formation of emergency friendships, often with people who in ordinary circumstances one might never have met. But, once the emergency-type procedures have been set in motion, the accompanying emergency friendships tend to generate instant intimacy, and with it, instant trust. The nuclear family has, in any case, come to rely more and more on friendship and less and less on kinship.

Lisa and Gwen met in the maternity ward after each had given birth to a first baby. Their immediate friendship ripened into a close one as soon as they realized that they lived within walking distance of one another. It was a friendship between the two women rather than between the two couples. Two-and-a-half years later both women had a second child, born in the same month. Lisa and her husband Bill had a staid marriage. Gwen and George had a turbulent one. When Gwen divorced George, after eight years of marriage, Lisa and Bill took care of her until a new home could be arranged. Gwen's presence in the household meant that it was possible for Lisa to go to Glasgow when her father had a sudden heart attack. It was while she was away that her best friend began an affair with her husband. 'It was,' said Gwen, 'one of those things that just happened.' Both Gwen and Bill felt 'bad about it' and when Lisa returned they decided to 'give it up', which they did until Gwen found a flat. The affair began again and only ended when Bill left Lisa. Gwen, who is now married to Bill, feels that Lisa 'never really loved Bill'. Lisa had complained about 'how boring he was', she had described him as a 'poor lover'; Bill thought Lisa was as cold as a fish. She wasn't 'such a good wife' herself. She never really 'appreciated' him. True, what Gwen and Bill had done to Lisa 'wasn't nice', they 'didn't feel good about it'. But Gwen is paying for it. 'Bill's family made me pay. They hardly have anything to do with me, even now.' (Gwen and Bill have been married for four years.)

The effectiveness, in terms of striking power, of the best friend or the friend of the Other Woman is well demonstrated by those women who later admitted that they went all out to be successful at cultivating a friendship with a wife solely because it was the one sure way of getting close to her husband. In those cases where the two women had been friends, both the husband and the Other Woman expected and received sympathy and, often, even admiration for the honesty and the courage that the force of romantic love had exacted from them.

The affair between Marion and Ian began twenty-five years ago when she was 28 and Ian was 38. Remarriage is as undesirable now as it was from the beginning. It was about four years before Ian's wife Jean was to suspect anything of a private relationship between her husband and her friend. By that time Marion was an experienced campaigner – in other words, Marion had been successfully engaged in the battle long before Jean was aware of having been attacked.

The first prong of Marion's tactics was to cultivate the friendship between herself and Jean. The second was to consolidate the relationship between the two men, and therefore between the two couples. Once they were a foursome, they could all spend more time together, playing golf or bridge, discussing the books they had all read, going to concerts, and taking holidays together.

The couples were well matched. The two women were of high and equal intelligence, the two men of great and equal wealth. Marion's husband Keith was devoted to her, and indeed Ian was a very good husband to Jean. Ian and Jean's sex life had diminished; he believed that since she had never really wanted sex, she didn't really miss it. Marion knew this to be untrue, but never said so. Jean had confided the story of an earlier affair to Marion. The reasons for Marion's silence offer certain insights into the nature of the Woman versus Woman conflict. Marion preferred Ian to maintain his (inaccurate) image of his wife as a woman who didn't need sex. This in turn meant that he would feel little guilt about his lack of sexual connection with his wife. Apart from that, however, if he did not see his wife as a sexual being, it was likely he would believe other men would see her in a light similar to his own. His sexual interest in his wife would not be revived by any jealousy on his part. Marion's silence extended beyond Jean's earlier affair. She did not state openly that she agreed that Jean had never liked sex, but confirmed that 'some women were probably like that'. Marion therefore managed not only to agree that Jean was sexless, but underlined it by implying that for many women, the sexless state was not so very unusual anyway.

However, although Marion had no wish to divorce her own husband, she could not help being terribly jealous of the relationship between Ian and his wife. Since they were together so often, she was a reluctant witness to that 'habit of tenderness that develops between a husband and a wife'. When after four years Jean began to be aware of the nature of the relationship between her husband and Marion, she retaliated by cooling the friendship. She, too, deployed silence; not a word was said about why matters were cooling. But bridge games became unpleasant, arrangements were cancelled at the last minute, and she was disagreeable to the point of hostility. Marion hoped for the friendship to continue, but their evenings together degenerated, and it was clear that Jean was not to be deflected. Marion and her own husband had long ago agreed that Jean was a 'jealous bitch who was even too idiotic to hide her jealousy'. Marion's husband believed that his wife had done nothing to merit Jean's jealousy, it was just that she was the jealous type.

Marion now feels that although she did not achieve an outright victory, she did achieve a victory of a sort, for if only in a *cinq à sept* fashion, she and Ian continue to meet. Complete victory was dependent on the regular foursome continuing their social meetings. She misses their joint activities. If Jean knows of their secret meetings she says nothing about it. But Marion believes that Jean, too, scored a victory of a sort; when she ended the friendship she got her own way.

Though Sue survived her best friend Joan's attack, she believes that the double betrayal had a very profound effect on her husband, Paul, an insurance broker. Whether or not he was unfaithful to her before then is of no significance, because even if he was, no real strain was put on the marriage. However, once Sue became suspicious of Joan, the texture of the marriage altered. Sue's clinging quest for reassurance, and Paul's vicious, impatient denials not only of his infidelity but of her rationality and even her sanity led to ugly scenes that often culminated in Paul's angry insistence, 'Ask Joan what is in your sick mind. Go ahead. Make a fool of yourself!' Which, of course, Sue could not do. Poor, child-like Joan, ten years older than Sue, who liked to say 'praps' instead of perhaps, who had seven children as well as a collection of Raggedy-Anne dolls, who had feet as large as Paul's, but who was so sensitive, so sad, so appealingly unhappy because her husband's drinking and vulgarity had made her suffer so. Joan was always on the telephone, always 'popping in', always there. Sue's coldness was met by Joan's tears, and, had she done anything wrong? Tears never reddened or puffed Joan's eyes. Instead they grew larger and bluer. But Sue found tears unbearably moving none the less. She could not, not ever, ever, *ever*, have borne to upset Joan. But though Sue saw as much as felt her own twelve-year marriage deteriorate, she said nothing to Joan.

Years later Sue came to understand the effect of Paul's

betrayal on his own psyche. For in betraying his wife with her best friend he had betrayed himself. The light went out of his wife and out of his life. He had put that light out, and could not forgive himself or anyone else, Sue included. At the time, however, Sue acted on instinct and formulated a strategy. She took what she knew to be a wild chance and gambled everything. She told Paul that she had to warn him about something she'd heard. She couldn't say if it was true or not, but she'd been told that Joan's husband knew about him, was furious, and planning to take violent action against him, and would make trouble for him at work too. Sue was only telling him about this because she felt it was only right to protect him. Of course, if he thought it would help, she herself would call on Joan's husband and tell him that although there had been vicious rumours about his wife and her husband they were not, and never had been, true. She stressed that even if it was all true, this is what she would say.

She says that part of her instinct told her that Paul was a coward – she unashamedly believes that most men are cowards – and that she knew he'd run for his life from a fight. Though immensely relieved, she was hardly surprised when Paul not only agreed to her idea, but told her how it had all begun. . . . Joan had phoned him on a Tuesday afternoon at work, about seven months previously, saying that she was suicidal, she had to talk to someone, she was going mad, and would he come over and just talk to her. When he arrived, the front door was open, Joan was pale and weeping uncontrollably in her bed. Naturally, he took her in his arms, to comfort her, and the rest followed and could not be helped. Sue understood and sympathized with his story and took him in her arms and comforted him, and the rest, as she says, could not be helped, either.

The next morning Sue suggested that, after seeing Richard, Joan's husband, she would have lunch with Joan. Joan would certainly not refuse – she had been trying to have lunch with Sue for ages. She then offered Paul what she termed serious advice from an old and trusted friend. It was simply this: under no circumstances should he speak to Joan until after both of Sue's meetings. This Paul accepted with alacrity.

Sue requested and was granted an urgent meeting with Richard. She told him about the rumours, but refused to name her informants. She also told him that she would be seeing Joan. Joan, she knew, was at that moment on her way to the restaurant, and there was no way that Richard could talk with her before she met Sue. For an awful moment Sue thought he would suggest lunching with both of them; and though he said he wished he could he also said he couldn't get away from the office – there was an important directors' meeting.

During the lunch Sue ate with gusto, while Joan didn't even pretend to try to eat. First, Sue told her all about her meeting with Richard and what she had said. Then she mentioned Joan's hysterical attack that Tuesday afternoon. She added that this lunch was Paul's idea. She said that Paul had begged her to see Richard, and then she opened her bag, took out more money than was needed, placed it on the table – and left.

That night Sue told Paul that she would wait for him for as long as it would take. She wouldn't dream of asking him not to see Joan, but she would prefer never to see either of them together again. She said that Joan had insisted that Paul had forced her, practically raped her, that Tuesday afternoon . . . which was precisely the sort of dirty lie she could not and would not accept. But Paul, it seemed, did not want to see Joan again, not ever. You mean, Sue laughed, not ever, ever, *ever*? And with that sort of humorous mockery of Joan, Sue consolidated her victory.

Sue's humorous mockery of her rival underlines an important factor in the Woman versus Woman conflict, namely the necessity of diminishing the Other Woman without diminishing the man.

Everyone who knew her tried to dissuade Patricia from marrying Simon. Patricia restored paintings, and had a small legacy. Simon, a sometime actor, swaggered when he walked, exposed his prematurely greying hairs on the chest Patricia adorned with gold chains, and wore a well-fitting toupé. His striking looks and openly flirtatious manner were extravagant enough to put few women off; those who fell for him fell hard and far, and Patricia was one of those. Though his handsome face retained something boyish, Simon looked older than he was; he looked closer to 40 than to 33. Patricia was 41, but her trendy dress and her long hair with its blonde highlights gave her the illusory look of a woman in her early thirties.

They were married, and Simon moved into Patricia's elegant, ultra-modern flat where she lived with her daughter, Fiona, 17, who was still at an expensive boarding school. Patricia's work made this possible. Fiona's father, Patricia's ex-husband, had moved to America and disappeared. The marriage went well, marred only by the fact that Simon was 'resting' – out of work – most of the time. Patricia worked at home, and perhaps it was because they spent too much time together or perhaps it was because Simon resolutely left all household duties to Patricia that, after about ten months, things began to deteriorate. They snapped at one another, Patricia began to look even older than she was, and Simon enrolled at an expensive gymnasium and went there every day.

It was at this time that Fiona, having completed her A-levels, came home. Patricia sent her to a secretarial school. Fiona went through a sudden delayed adolescence. She was impertinent to her mother and even more impertinent to Simon. She came to breakfast in a flimsy nightgown, rushed around the flat in a towel, that sort of thing. Patricia couldn't believe what was happening; she believed it even less when she saw Simon looking at her own daughter with that familiar look she knew so well, and which everyone had warned her against. Their lovemaking decreased.

Patricia asked herself what she had done to deserve this – her first husband had deserted her, and since then all she had ever wanted was the right to live her own life. She may have looked young and glamorous, vital and energetic, but she had worked hard at being these things. She'd been a conscientious mother, and not once in all those five years after her husband had left her, and before Fiona had gone away to school, had she gone out before Fiona had fallen asleep. No, not once. She thought she was going mad – it wasn't possible, it couldn't be happening.

She never accused either of them outright, but daily there were ugly scenes, when Patricia would feel her face flush and her voice turn harsh, and then she would weep. And yet, when both of them left, she was hardly surprised. Fiona and Simon are in Australia now, living in the outback somewhere. Patricia receives the occasional card, but has no idea how they live. Fiona sent her a photograph of her baby son. She said they had called him Patrick, in honour of his grandmother.

Brenda Maddox, in *Step-Parenting*, says, 'Incest may be the last taboo in a permissive society.' As long as the emphasis on things sexual continues to rise, it seems more and more likely that 'youthful' mothers of, say, 35, struggling to look as young as their daughters, will find themselves engaged in the Woman versus Woman conflict. It is a terrifyingly tricky problem for a mother to handle; if she warns her daughter against possible sexual advances from her stepfather, she reduces whatever little trust her daughter may have had in men. However, Patricia believes that this is what she should have done. She bitterly regrets not having talked to her daughter, woman-to-woman, not having told her what she had always known, but repressed, about the way in which men, especially older men, can be sexually aroused by the body of a nubile young girl, no matter who she is, no matter if he doesn't even know her.

Patricia *never* talks of her experience. She heard that *Woman versus Woman* was being written, and wanted others to have the benefit of her insight.

11

Stepwives: the conflict continues

Almost every woman who is 'promoted' to wife believes that in some important way she is superior to her predecessor. This is as true of the teenager whose sole value to her new husband rests on the fact that she is still untried, untested and unformed as it is of the Other Woman whose life-style and personal history is comparable to that of the defeated wife. For, however distinctive and whatever their duration, the qualities of the defeated wife have now been *proved* (by her husband's defection) to be inferior to those of her successor. Even in these enlightened days it seems that marriage, or rather the offer of marriage, is still held to be the ultimate measure of supremacy in the Woman versus Woman conflict. Too often it is also the means by which the Other Woman assesses her own worth – after all, her success is entirely dependent on someone else's failure.

Frequently the victor, or replacement wife, assumes something of a proprietorial interest in her husband's reject. Many feel a sense of connectedness, not quite a fusion, though a familiarity bordering on intimacy, with the displaced wife. Frequently her involvement with her predecessor long outlasts that of her husband, even when alimony and other like complications are absent. The Other Woman can't help knowing that the result was in her favour; the wife was abandoned for her and the family destroyed on her behalf. If she now has the privileged role of wife, a little bit of *noblesse oblige* is not altogether inappropriate, certainly as far as the family's remnants, the children, are concerned. Speaking of her 14-year-old stepdaughter, Sue, Beryl said, 'She's a slut, like her mother. The least I can do for Stan is to make sure that she has some taste. But she gets herself up like a tart, like her mother!'

Though discarded, something of the predecessor's presence endures, if only as evidence of the husband's previous poor taste and still poorer judgement. Encouraged and even supported by her predecessor's failings, the successor absorbs something of that persona into her own. For whatever else the discarded wife may or may not have been, *she could not keep her man.*

> 'He's 45 now. We've been married for three years. But I tell him I hope he's past it now, that he won't leave me the way he left her. He never thinks about her. I keep wondering why she couldn't keep him? Don't want to make the same mistake,'

said Nell, whose husband had left his wife six months after he and Nell had met.

At 63, Arthur's wife Molly could well have been cast as the little old lady who bullies officials and gets her own way. At least that is how she struck Rebecca, replacement Rebecca, 19, even though Rebecca had only seen Molly once. Molly's snow-white hair in its tight curls under a beret or a woollen cap made her look older than her years. It was hard to imagine her ever having been young. Arthur, a history professor, was 62, but looked younger; tennis was his passion and it was on the tennis court that he and Rebecca first met. His children, two daughters, were in their late thirties; and when he left Molly he announced that if they did not accept Rebecca he would not accept them.

Rebecca's chief anxiety about Molly was that no one she knew should ever see her, because, if they did, she would have 'died of shame'. Molly was so old-fashioned, she had thick 'piano' legs, was plump, and really looked as if she belonged to an old people's home. Arthur himself had said that she had an 'old woman's smell'. To say that Rebecca felt superior is to say too little – Rebecca felt superior beyond compare. She was more concerned with her own rebellion than with Molly's forty years of marriage. Molly was as obsolete as an old car for which spare parts had long been unavailable. Arthur and Molly's divorce is still pending; he and Rebecca have been together for just on a year. Molly is more like Arthur's *mother* than his wife, which is why Rebecca feels it is only natural for him to visit her from time to time.

The objective of the divorce mechanism is to effect a clear severing and a clean break. If it does not always achieve its objective, it is because laws cannot effect amnesia. But when the remarriage is the direct outcome of the Woman versus Woman conflict, the lengthened connection between the two women is hardly to be wondered at. The successor very often dominates the mind and heart of her predecessor long after her very existence has been erased from her successor's mind. But her predecessor experiences the kind of unrequited hate that lasts long enough to make itself felt, and more than one long-standing replacement wife has been forced to confront her long-forgotten predecessor at a husband's deathbed or at his funeral.

> 'He cut his teeth on me. We were married for twenty odd years, and then he left me for her. I was the one who struggled with him, who worked with him, and then she came along and got all the benefits of *my* work. They travelled all the time. The alimony I got at the time of the divorce (twenty-eight years ago) was not cost-of-living-indexed and it's a pittance now. We had three children, we'd had four, but one of them died when she was a baby, two of our children had their own children, and so we even had grandchildren in common. We used to see one another, sometimes: but he was terrified of her finding out.

When he was dying, we went to the hospital to see him. She couldn't take that, she said he couldn't take the strain, said he should be left alone with his real family. How often have you seen him in the last twenty-eight years, she wanted to know. So I told her. She said I was lying and told me that he used to tremble whenever he received a letter from me, said it took him days before he could get up the courage to open it. She said I could easily have remarried, but that I hadn't only because I wanted to bleed them dry. She knew that the terms of our divorce agreement were that I would continue to receive my alimony for as long as I lived, even after his death.

'He told me he wanted to see me. So I used to go to the hospital at 6 a.m. She didn't know. We did a deal with the nurses. When he died she had the impertinence to force her son to come to see me to ask me not to go to his funeral. Why not? I said. He was the father of my children as much as he was your father. You'll see that when you see the will. You've got a shock coming to you, I said. We'd never met until the hospital. Of course we went to the funeral, and to the wake. Our grandchildren, too. We mourned him no less than they. She didn't want her friends to see me. She wanted all their friends to think he'd never had another wife or another family. She didn't want anyone to know I'd ever existed. I introduced myself to most of the people who were there.'

The emanations of a predecessor tend to be experienced far more acutely by women than by men. Curiously, though, men tend to understand and sympathize with this sort of attitude to a predecessor even though few new husbands have any difficulty in living in the house that was once lived in and decorated by their predecessor, or even sleeping in the same bed in which their predecessor had once slept. It seems a man is not nearly as concerned as a woman to leave his own imprint on his surroundings. A husband may mark or stake out a study or a workshop as his sovereign territory within the household but the rest is usually his wife's domain.

'I don't mind living in his house,' said Max, 'but I hate those photograph albums.' Men, too, are concerned with memories of others locked up in records, films, pieces of porcelain, a certain chair, etc., but they are not nearly as driven as the woman who feels she must change the wallpaper or the furniture of a predecessor. The new wife longs to eradicate her memory, and so has new furnishings, and perhaps, depending on her age, new children. (Of course this is not the *only* reason why second wives increase their family.) Beverley, however, said,

> 'Look, I already had two of my own kids. I thought I had completed my family. I was 34, and if I hadn't have got divorced I wouldn't have had another child. I had had an abortion. He had *his* two kids. I wanted *us* to have *our* child.'

Even the very unobservant would not help noticing the adoration and the reverence with which Ursula viewed her husband Miles. There was something about the way in which they were connected that brought to mind an invisible umbilical cord, as if each had been created for the other, like the ancient Ming vases. Their glances met, and intersected fleetingly but frequently; reassurance was constantly sought and just as constantly given. Their hands appeared to describe the same definite, rather than graceful, movements, for their long sturdy fingers gave the illusion of being interchangeable. There was nothing of the Darby and Joan about them; sensuality had always been their mainspring. This had probably been obvious from the very beginning of their association, but what made it so striking, almost shocking, so that one was compelled to notice it, was their age. Miles was 70 and Ursula 66. Neither of them tried to look younger. Ursula was tall and broad, and wore her soft, shiny grey hair with a fringe and reaching her collar. Miles's hair reached his collar, too, though his was a harder grey than hers. They had been living together for twenty-six years, but had known one another for fourteen years before that. Their only child, now 24, was born when Ursula was 43.

Their only child was not his only child, for by the time he met Ursula he was already the father of four children; by the time Ursula gave birth to their child, she had had several abortions. But Ursula and Miles have never been married; she has taken his name by deed poll. Miles has not seen his wife, Geraldine, since the day of that single flare-up, the day something in him snapped, the day he left her forever. One of Ursula's letters had gone astray and when it found its way into Geraldine's hands she made the mistake of confronting him with an angry scene, and so it was that something snapped, and he went to live with Ursula, never to return.

Miles is a sensitive man, and could not bear the suffering he caused Geraldine. And he is as conscious of that suffering now as he was when it all began. Geraldine did not want to be his divorced wife: she wanted to remain his wife which Miles and Ursula felt was the very least that they could do for her. And of course, because this sort of thing came naturally to both of them, they did their combined best to make Geraldine's life as comfortable, materially, as possible. Though Miles is a distinguished academic their financial resources were limited, and Geraldine's wellbeing has been at the cost of considerable material hardship to Ursula.

Twice a week, every week, for the past twenty-six years, Geraldine writes to her husband, Miles. And once a week, every week, Miles replies. But though her letters distressed him, he felt under an obligation to read them, and to suffer. After fifteen years, Ursula came to his rescue: it was decided that she would make a précis of the letters and, at the same time, censor them of their emotional content. During these twenty-six years Geraldine has seen her husband three times. Once she saw him trudging along in a nearby street, kicking the autumn leaves; another time she glimpsed him leaving a pub, and on the third occasion she attended one of his public lectures. She had not approached him; she doubted whether he would have recognized her. She has also seen him on the television screen and heard him on the radio.

Geraldine lives 'a pretty reclusive life'. But, as Ursula says, 'she is a very keen observer of life; she reads the newspapers and comments on global and local matters.' Her letters are interesting, Ursula admits, and very well written, but a fearful chore. In all these twenty-six years her letters have not once made any mention of Ursula, nor of their son, who is now 24. Not once in all those years has Ursula seen how Miles addresses his wife; she does not know whether he calls her dearest, or my dearest, or, worse still, my darling. Nor does she know how he concludes his weekly letter – does he end on a note of love, as Geraldine does? Geraldine begins with some variation on 'my love'; she writes of how she misses him, of how she loves him; she speaks of him as her husband, of herself as his wife. So intimately has Ursula shared the life of her predecessor that she knows the status of the bulbs in her cellar. And yet Geraldine has no notion of Ursula's deep bond with her; she does not know that her letters are read, and then, like a scientific paper, summarized for her husband's inspection and reply. Ursula's life is bound up with Miles, with her son, and with Geraldine. She takes consolation, even now, from Miles's statement that Geraldine 'was not a very sexual woman'. Just lately, however, Geraldine's presence has become less burdensome, less oppressive, because for the past two years or so she has at last been excluded from Ursula's dreams.

And yet Ursula is in a kind of daily communion, almost a harmony, though very much in the way of an *alter ego*, with the woman who, as Ursula said, rightly knows her to be her enemy.

It is odd how, even when the peace is made and the treaty signed, the Woman versus Woman conflict lengthens.

Most men find neither the ghost nor the presence of a predecessor as a threat, which leads us to a further obvious but little stated difference between men and women, namely, that men do not assess other men in their social circle in terms of their potential threat quotient as women (instinctively, perhaps) tend to do.

'Now that I'm married, I see things differently, especially since Amanda was born,' said Jess, whose marriage to Vincent took place the day after his divorce from Theresa became final.

> 'I think if I had known Theresa I would not have been so certain that Vince and I were made for one another. I don't think they were as unhappy as he made out. He's no angel to live with, believe me! If I ask him to pick up his own socks, for example, he accuses me of being just like Theresa. And then I say that he's so difficult, it's no wonder he and Theresa couldn't get on.
>
> 'She's with us all the time, not physically, but *there*, if you know what I mean. She just about phones him to come over and change a bulb. He feels so guilty about her and about the kids that he runs to do her bidding. I hate it when he even talks to her on the telephone and I'm miserable when he sees her. I'm sure it's got to the point that he doesn't tell me every time he sees her. There's nothing I can do about it. Our low standard of living is more or less because of her. She could remarry. She's a good-looking woman; but why should she risk losing our financial support?
>
> 'I used to be his secretary, before we got married. That was how we met. I seem to have a thing about his secretaries – this is the third one he's had since our marriage, and I was rude to her as well. She'd come here for dinner, and I walked into the kitchen and the two of them were chatting while he washed some glasses. I began banging things about, and as soon as Vince left the room, I told her to keep her hands off my husband. The poor girl didn't know what I was talking about. I'm hung-up about this, I know. I'm sure it's because I got him away from Theresa so easily. Of course he agonized before he left her,

but *he actually did leave her*. I can't get that out of my mind. I'll never feel secure with Vince, never!'

Jess is a fairly typical example of the second wife who knows she owes her marriage to the vulnerability of all marriages. In her useful book, *How to Survive as a Second Wife*, Maggie Drummond notes that 'second marriages collapse at twice the rate of first ones.' The lives of most second wives are affected by the former lives of their husbands; second marriages frequently collapse under the burden of the omnipresent complications of the history in which the present wife had no part, but which inevitably becomes as well, if not better, known than her own. It is his past that she feels, too often, more acutely than her own, for however well known that past becomes it remains mysterious. And it is the combination of the known and the mysterious that infects her present.

Still other second or third wives are jealous of their predecessors, even when there is no good reason, even when the husband swears he 'hates the bitch.' Of course some second wives come to terms with their husband's ex-wife. Pat decided to be 'big enough' to overcome her hatred of Cynthia, for the children's sake. This way Robbie is 'able to be more of a father to them. I'm lucky that Cynthia cooperates. My sister's ex's wife won't allow him to have anything to do with her!'

Replacement wives, needless to say, are more than ordinarily aware of the potential threat quotient, not least because they have direct experience of a potential threat being turned into an effective danger. Sometimes the husband who has been common to both (or all) wives has the same sort of unifying effect as shared experiences. But when a third contender arrives and eventually overcomes the second wife, the first and second wives have defeat in common, and it seems a shared defeat is capable of igniting fusion qualities of the most uncommon kind. If the resultant harmony is not quite as deadly as its proponents would wish, it is at least comforting. Linked in defeat, they embrace one another in tears and atonement in a way that would be inconceivable to two similarly defeated husbands. Though all is far from forgiven and still further from forgotten, the two women may become bosom friends, if only for a while.

They may even plot together to eliminate the third, each under the false illusion that the other has given up all hope of being a contender; sometimes the husband chooses again the first, sometimes the second, sometimes he chooses both, and sometimes neither. That it is his choice is of little consequence here. More to the point, however, is that, great harmony notwithstanding, each conceals her availability (to the man) from the other.

Another linking phenomenon occurs when the first wife and the third join against the second. The first is grateful to the third not only for having freed him from the terrible second, but for having dealt to the second the same deadly blow that was dealt to her. It is a revenge of the most exquisite sort; since it has been effected by another and therefore purified, it is quintessential retribution.

So the Woman versus Woman conflict continues; the replacement wife insists that the children have been poisoned against her as they have been against their father, as all too often they have been. But even those displaced wives who have made a conscious, almost superhuman, and successful effort not to influence their children against their father are held accountable for the children's resentment towards the new stepparent.

And even in those instances when the children do not wish to sabotage the new marriage, they sabotage it anyway. Their need for financial support may mean that there are insufficient funds for the support of the replacement's as yet unborn children. Besides, their very existence is permanent evidence of a past serious failure. Again it is necessary to stress that we are here concerned with the remarriage that is a direct consequence of the Woman versus Woman conflict. Even those replacement wives who were never involved in the Woman versus Woman conflict experience great difficulty in coping at close and intimate quarters with another woman's children. This may take the form of being kinder and more solicitous of her stepchildren than of her own. Children usually present something of a problem to those in their charge, but stepchildren usually present a problem of a more awkward order.

Two sets of stepchildren mean that the family must constantly alter its shape. Weekends, for example, may consist of eight instead of four – the father's visiting children are guests instead of inhabitants of *his* house – but though guests, they feel they have more claim on him than do his resident stepchildren, and no less of a claim than his own new children. The children tend to divide into factions and so it is not unknown for the concomitant strife to lead to the first lot of children drawing alongside the former wife, and turning into former children.

However, not all fathers abandon their young, and very often favour their own over their stepchildren, and many remarriages fail on this account. This does not mean that the defeated wife rises in victory. There is a multiplicity of defeats; instead of one there are now three.

The continual invasions of the guest-children mean that the family is never quite an independent entity and therefore not quite whole. Where the replacement wife is 'sensitive' about her predecessor as well as her predecessor's children (as even Nancy Reagan after more than thirty years is still said to be) she is none the less still compelled to suffer the presence of her enemy's spies in her own house. Some replacement wives become paranoid over details such as meals, and watch each guest-child's mouthfuls for evidence of yet more sedition. The displaced wife for whom she once had so much contempt is now able to sit in judgement on her, and she will go to almost any lengths to conceal any evidence of marital difficulty from the all-seeing eyes of the child spy.

Now although the replacement wife chooses to believe that she would not be in her present position unless her husband's former marriage had been at breaking point anyway, the children are evidence that but for her intervention the family might not have broken up. This might even activate the conscience that she feels she has no cause for and is not supposed to have, anyway. Those all-seeing eyes of the guest-children activate more than guilt, for sometimes the stepmother – who is not yet a mother – sees that though the children may not be innocent, they are still children and therefore lovable, and the father who could bring himself to desert them is suddenly less than lovable. The guest-children make her broody, and at the same time hyperprotective of her own unborn children, and then the man who proved his love and made her his wife is left behind. Father-deprivation is for other people's children: she dare not take a chance with her own unborn children's lives. She sends him back to his former wife, sometimes too late, for the children already have their own new resident stepfather.

The continuation, after the victory, of the Woman versus Woman conflict bewilders most men, largely because they are much more trusting of other men than women are of other women. Perhaps they are more trusting because they can afford to be – they know that it is almost embarrassingly easy to take their pick from among all those who clamour to console.

12

The man in the middle

The happily married man who has never had an affair of one sort or another is almost a non-conformist. The acceptability of male infidelity is hardly new, and lust, whether consummated or otherwise, has always been with us, as even that happiest of husbands, Jimmy Carter, admitted.

Needless to say, neither every infidelity nor every affair leads automatically to the Woman versus Woman conflict. Such a conflict, it is safe to say, is the last thing to occur to most married men. The husband usually imagines that if there is to be a war, it will be his war – the war to be waged with himself and with his wife. And because it is unlikely that he is familiar with the Woman versus Woman conflict, he will be unaware that he will not only be at its centre, but will be the territory over which it will be fought. The majority of the husbands in this study saw themselves at the centre of a triangle; few suspected that they could be at the centre of a complicated conflict between two women. (A few husbands, however, were only too well aware of the conflict and went as far as to ask the new women in their lives to fight it out with their wives.) But the revelation of the Woman versus Woman conflict brought with it all manner of unexpected responses, ranging from being excessively flattered to being excessively enraged. The following extracts exemplify some of these reactions:

'I never knew my wife had the guts!' said George Tomlinson (35, a television engineer) of his wife Mabel, who had taken it on herself to visit the parents of 21-year-old Jill.

'I didn't know how much my wife cared,' said Richard (53, an accountant), of his wife Sue, 38, who had faced his confession with tears as well as sympathy.

'Normally Meg wouldn't say boo to a goose. But she went and poured a pint over Jennifer,' said Fred (28, a carpenter), of his wife Lily.

'Gloria went to see the headmaster of Sue's (my girlfriend) school. Gloria was 22 at the time, and pregnant. I thought I might kill her, so I left her. Then Sue's parents talked her out of me. That happened five years ago, and Gloria and I have two kids now,' said Colin (27, a taxi driver).

'My girlfriend persuaded my wife to take me back. She was a good deal younger than me – she met a guy of her own age,' said Bernard (51, a furniture salesman).

'My wife went to beg Nancy to give me up for the sake of our kids. Just like I was a box of chocolates. I wasn't having any of that. I've never forgiven my wife for it,' said Harry (47, a plumber).

Since it is clear that every infidelity does not result in a Woman versus Woman conflict, it might be helpful to make some reference to the way the married man tends to relate to those women outside his family with whom he comes into contact.

Anyone who has suffered the disproportionate, inordinate and incalculable power of romantic/sexual love knows that it is a force which overwhelms both the mind and the character. It annihilates religion, reason, respect and rationality. Though it is said to be an affair of the heart, it engenders heartlessness, and it converts friendships into enmity. The obstacles that stand in its way heighten its power. It is a force that confers a sense of deathless permanence.

Everyone who is not in the grip of such a force knows – or ought to know – that it cannot sustain itself. But the state of the marriage notwithstanding, most husbands face an agonizing dilemma as soon as they begin to consider defecting to the Other Woman. In a torment of conflicting yet converging emotions, ecstasy clashes with anguish, responsibility with danger, guilt with rage. But sexual or aphrodisiacal ecstasy is both a faith and a justification in itself; the problem is that the husband has to search out and find (and if necessary create) other less obvious, but more sensible justifications for his impending defection. He looks at his wife, his children, and wonders how he can even contemplate hurting them so badly; and then a little later, or even at the same time, he wonders how they dare stand in his way – he only has one life, after all. At the same time he wants to do what is best for himself. He loves his wife, he loves his children, he is not a gambler, but yet he is ready to gamble. Will he be happier with the Other Woman? Certainly he will be happier than he is now. His home has become a battlefield: there are daily scenes, many of which he provokes – he needs to be more convinced about how much happier he is sure to be. At least he'll have some respite from that beaten-looking woman with the reproachful stare who is doing her best to make him feel even more guilty, even more miserable. If only she'd throw him out, if only she'd force him to choose, she'd make it all so much easier for him.

He notes, with relief, that things are becoming rough at home. He's said a few cruel things to his wife, and she took the bait, the silly fool. How could he ever have believed he'd been happy with such a silly woman? Well, even if he was happy, he's not happy now – indeed he's as miserable as he had hoped to be.

His wife has said some pretty unforgivable things about his girlfriend. She doesn't care about his girlfriend's suffering in all of this – she even *wants* her to suffer. But he'll protect his girlfriend from his wife, whatever happens. His girlfriend wants him, and his wife wants him, and he's in the middle. Still, they both want him. It's very flattering, of course; which one should he take, the licorice or the peppermint? How can he choose? He has both, and he has only one life.

The dilemma forces him to make things at home as difficult as possible, and sometimes, though rarely, even at the lovenest. He becomes irritable, bitter, ill-tempered, cruel – in short, the family or the marriage has an enemy in its midst, and an enemy waiting on the sidelines.

He knows, in the deepest recesses of his mind, that the affair has run out of control and consumed him. He knows, and cannot forgive his wife. Which means that while there is both ecstasy and torment, tragedy waits in the wings. Because, no doubt about it, it would be tragic, the destruction of his family. Besides, what would happen to *him*? Could he bear it?

In these circumstances his work begins to suffer. He's abstracted, preoccupied – he takes too much time over his lunch hour (he's meeting his girlfriend), he jumps when the phone rings (he hopes it's his girlfriend), he takes whole days off (surely they are entitled to spend a day together?). His girlfriend understands his dilemma, and sympathizes with his difficulties. She believes he's thinking about – and working towards – a divorce.

He's anxious and, strung as he is between one meeting and the next, the pitch of his excitement is almost excruciatingly constant. For his body is used, exercised, stretched, and so is his mind – he has to remember his lies and balance his excuses. Something – or someone – will have to give.

Nothing is as it was; everything is more acute, even his powers of observation. At home, he is not quite an outsider, nor yet an alien, but an observer. The innocence of his children is intoxicating and intolerable, precious and unbearably burdensome. He cannot endure the harm he contemplates for them; but he has only one life. Surely, under the tyranny of ecstasy he has the right to a second life with a new wife?

He observes with his newly educated eyes his present wife, who used to be rather pretty; even his girlfriend remarked how pretty she must have been. She's 33 now, but looks older – old, actually, after three children, it's not her fault. Still, his girlfriend, 30, and a mother of two, looks like a teenager.

The state of the marriage has little to do with the compulsion felt by every defecting husband to make comparisons between the two women. There may be glaring differences, of course, but again and again husbands referred to qualities in their wives, their girlfriends, or in both that he had not noticed until his attention had been drawn to them. The pressure to make a decision intensifies his need to compile a roster of his wife's failings. Of course there are cases where the marriage is so bad and the relationship so sour that the husband has no need to add to an already overflowing list. But even this does not necessarily mean that there will be no conflict, and several husbands and numerous Other Women reported that the wife's role in the Woman versus Woman conflict was simply 'to behave more like a human being'. This sort of change for the better was enough to make the husband decide against defection, or to continue with both, the marriage and the Other Woman.

It is safe to say that all those husbands who were in a healthy marriage were certain, if not determined to ensure, that the affair would be a short-lived, transitory experience. A surprisingly large number claimed that they had not taken the initiative in beginning the affair. 'I was taken unawares'; 'She caught me off guard'; 'She told me I turned her on'; 'I wasn't looking for trouble'; 'She seduced me. By the time I realized that, I was already married to her.' For some it was one of a series of encounters, for others it was the first such encounter. But the one aspect that was common to all was the whole-hearted belief that even if the brief encounter turned into a longer one, it would never turn into anything serious enough to rock the marriage. There was always the risk of discovery, but that was only a calculated risk which anyway could be minimized by the use of maximum discretion. *But it would not in itself merit enough importance to cause any sort of disturbance to the marriage.* And then, because the instant intimacy was as gratifying and as warming and as unexpected as a cup of instant hot soup outdoors on a raw and windy day, it was even better than the real thing. Certainly it was different, and for a while at least, he would need more – and not less – of the same. What was going to be at most, and at best, nothing other than pure sex, turned into more than sex, and because it was mixed with the distillation of all his known and unknown emotions, it was love. He had fallen in love, and he had not wanted to, and it was no one's fault.

At any rate he had lost control; it was too soon or too late to reach for the brake. It seemed there would never be enough of those heights he reached so endlessly, so miraculously. And because there was too much to lose to bear thinking about, he suspended thought and, as one computer engineer put it, 'embraced madness'. Did his wife know? He and the Other Woman speculated endlessly – whether he should tell his wife, *how* he should tell her. The mystery added to his ecstasy, and strengthened it. How would his wife take it? How would she respond? But then all that potential hurt and destruction and tragedy would be in the name of love, that noblest of all causes. 'I thought that if I could even think of breaking up my family, it was only because I really was hopelessly in love!'

For the terrible price, leaving his family, would also be his terrible sacrifice, which very sacrifice would in a sense define its necessity. Of course, he loved his wife, once – he loves her now, he will always love her – but certainly he never felt anything like this! Life was less complicated then, and it is as if the measure of his present life complicated as it is by responsibilities and experiences is also the measure of his greater, and more complex, love.

Ecstasy makes its own laws and, according to scores of formerly happily married husbands, one of them is the loss of senses. Sadly, perhaps, many of those who lose their senses are condemned to finding them again.

The following phrases, usually used between 'If only my wife had realized that . . .' and '. . . then *she* might have saved us', crystallize the dilemma of the ecstasy:

'I was powerless'; 'I'd lost my senses'; 'I was cunt-struck'; 'I'd gone mad'; 'My brains had descended to my balls'; 'I thought I'd invented sex'; 'Outside of bed the Other Woman bored me (I knew that, I didn't care)'; 'I only *thought* I was in love with her'; 'I'd done my mind.'

Much of this sounds pretty adolescent. It's the old, old story of mistaking chemistry for compatibility, of believing that sexual fulfilment is not only eternal fulfilment, but makes every other activity fulfilling as well. Incidentally, a striking number of those husbands who did not defect said it was because of their wife's perception of what can happen to a man when he loses his senses.

How, you might ask, does the happily married man come to be in the midst of the Woman versus Woman conflict in the first place? Happiness does not confer immunity; it has never been armour-like protection and, contrary to orthodoxy, the healthy marriage need not be going through a 'bad patch' for its defences to be lowered. Even an ideal marriage is not impenetrable. An ideal husband, like an ordinary husband, has to be inordinately strong, not to say obstinate, if he is to refuse, rather than resist, all that which is so freely on offer. Although the pursuit of men by women has lost some of its subtlety, men have not yet developed an acceptable or easy pattern of refusal. The man who rejects a casual sexual invitation risks having his virility called into question, the way a woman who accepts a casual sexual invitation risks having her virtue called into question. Men are not expected to refuse. The art, skill and strategy of refusal is excluded from the family syllabus for boys, whereas it has long been a mandatory requirement for girls. At any rate, now that women are liberated instead of 'fast' or 'easy', emancipated men are only beginning to learn how to refuse gracefully.

Clearly, then, heterosexual men are not yet in the habit of refusing an open sexual advance. A case in point is James Cook, 38, married for fourteen years, a solicitor on the staff of an electronics company. Up until that business lunch with one of the directors of his company, James Cook would have described himself as happily married. Lunch was at the usual sort of elegant restaurant that handles the usual sort of expense account and facilitates the usual sort of talk over the usual sort of problems. James now swears that he can't remember whether or not he even noticed Anita who was lunching at a nearby table; what he does remember is the moment when the waiter offered him two brandies and a business card addressed to him. The card simply said, 'Would love to meet you, hope you enjoy the Courvoisier!' It would have been unmanly to refuse. James was almost unbearably flattered; his director beamed his admiration and so, over coffee and cognac, it all began. That an affair was neither something he wanted nor sought seems irrelevant now. James knows that he cannot live without Anita; nothing else counts.

Anita is 30 and a fashion buyer. She has introduced him to whole new worlds. She is a career woman, she can more than hold her own with any man, but even so James marvels at the courage with which she made that first advance.

The experience of James Cook and others like him led one husband to conclude that the 'hunted have become the hunters'. The pursuit of women by men is as old as evolution, and so it ought not to be surprising that the technique and the manner of that pursuit has evolved with the times. And yet it is still surprising, still shocking, and even those men and women who endorse equality and liberty continue to be taken unawares. Anita, needless to say, would hardly have marvelled at James's courage if he had offered her that card and those liqueurs.

If women are now able to pursue men more openly than ever before, they are also far more daring than men ever were. Consider, for example, Betty who followed John into his hotel room at a convention they were both attending. She had given him no prior warning of her intentions; nothing even vaguely suggestive had passed between them. They were both on their way to their rooms on the same floor, and as he opened his door, saying a polite goodnight, she slipped past him. Whereas a woman in his position would probably have responded with fear and anger, especially if nothing sexual had been present in their conversation, John greeted it with surprised bewilderment. Betty walked towards the bed, stood beside it, and began to loosen her buttons, saying that she thought he might like to make love to her. If James had done the same thing, Betty most likely would have screamed. Shocked into silence, John was far from screaming. Meanwhile, Betty rightly took his silence for assent as the bewildered James watched her slowly undress. James, 35 and until then utterly faithful, made love to her twice within forty minutes, and less than an hour after she had entered his room. Betty began to dress, told him that she had really needed that, and asked if he'd mind if she came back the following night.

Steve and Anne Williamson had bought a house believing that their flat had been sold. But the sale of the flat had fallen through. They were anxious about selling the flat, and Steve, 42 and a furniture salesman, was certain that he was more likely to effect a sale than anyone else. He advertised the flat by word of mouth, and one of his colleagues who thought he might be interested said he would send his wife, Sally, to view it. Steve had met Sally once or twice, a pretty woman in her early thirties who had seemed rather shy. Sally arrived on time, made the usual sort of polite enquiry about Steve's wife, Anne, and was told that she was at the new house trying to get things in order. Whereupon Sally moved towards him, threw her arms about him, and told him that she wanted him to make love to her. She disengaged her arms to raise her skirt, pressed against him once more, and Steve very quickly realized that she was wearing no underwear. They were still in the small hall of Steve's flat, and less than a minute had passed since he had closed the front door. The following two hours were spent in the kind of lovemaking that Steve had not even read about. He discovered that Sally was a versatile virtuoso, who extracted from him the kind of performances that surpassed even his adolescent fantasies.

The flat was sold to someone else but, seven months later, the affair continues. Steve is constantly on edge; he finds a secret life difficult to live, but says he is unable to give her up. Sally confessed that she had always found him attractive – that was why she had jumped at the chance of being alone with him. Sally's husband is morose and withdrawn and in a constant bad temper. She and Steve laugh a lot when they are together. Steve believes he is in love with Sally, and though they have not yet spent a whole night together, Sally is beginning to think they should 'stop before they get too involved' – neither of them wants to 'hurt Anne' – but Steve can't begin to contemplate 'giving up Sally'. Meanwhile the two couples have grown 'friendly' with each other. Sally has confided her difficulties with her husband to Anne who feels sorry for her, and often talks to Steve about 'poor Sally'.

'Poor Sally' has already made considerable gains in the Woman versus Woman conflict, since if Anne ever finds out about their affair, her hurt combined with the self-blame at not having guessed and the feeling that she has been fooled will turn her into a mindless, crazed adversary, which will make it all too easy for Steve to leave her for Sally.

The following example concerns an Other Woman, Alice, who was ready to 'look after' and to nurse her married man, Keith, because she believed she was better able to do so than his wife, Elizabeth, who was considerably older. Also, it was a way of proving her superior usefulness over that of his wife.

The Woman versus Woman conflict in this case has endured for twenty years, and though the two women have never met, a *modus vivendi* has been established. Elizabeth was unable to dispute the Other Woman's superior physical strength and did not wish to subject her ailing husband to any kind of additional pressure. Keith did not tell her who would be taking care of him, and they did not mention his regular holiday companion. It is probable that the Other Woman and her married man have discussed his wife far more frequently than the other way round. Keith and Alice were in the habit of going away together, once a year, for seventeen days. Elizabeth accepted this; she still had a full-time husband and all the status that went along with it. Each woman waited for him to make a final decision, each waited for the other to give him an ultimatum, and the conflict continued because neither woman had the smallest intention of giving way to the other. On both sides of the three-sided entanglement, each victory, each minor defeat, was measured against the man in the middle. The illness, like the holidays, equalled a victory for one and a defeat for the other.

Every morning, for twenty years, when he awoke, Keith telephoned Alice, just as he telephoned her last thing every night. About twelve years ago, Alice moved her flat to be nearer to Keith, and fell into the habit of driving him to work. Alice had visited the marital flat only once, twenty years before, at a cocktail party where it had all begun. Keith responded well to Alice's ministrations, and returned to Elizabeth, and their lives soon fell back into shape, with Elizabeth driving him to work every day. But one morning Keith told Alice that Elizabeth was ill, and that the doctor was with her. About an hour later, he telephoned her, distraught, saying that he had just been told that Elizabeth had died. Alice left her work, fetched him, took him home, and once again entered the flat she had last seen twenty years earlier.

Since Alice had outlived, if not outwitted, her rival, it seemed likely that after a decent interval her long-awaited marriage would take place. But it was not to be; Keith died six weeks later. And when Alice went to his funeral, Keith's daughter thanked her for having attended.

Many another Other Woman, though for different reasons, has found that the death of her married man's wife did not automatically lead to his remarriage to her, but to someone else.

The following excerpts from conversations with husbands whose wives' campaigns had been successful are highly illuminating. Again and again these men paid homage to their wives for their 'tact' and 'understanding', for not 'losing her cool' for 'not bitching about my girlfriend', for having been 'clever', a 'real woman for not belittling me but for understanding me instead'. Many men said this had resulted in 'stronger', 'happier' and 'better' marriages.

And yet, while these very men acknowledged and indeed paid tribute to their wives' role – or, as they readily conceded, their wives' campaign – in the Woman versus Woman conflict, almost all of them admitted that they would not have been capable of exercising anything like the same degree of control if it had been the other way round: 'I would have been furious. I'd have told her to go'; 'I'd have given up. I wouldn't have thought of fighting'; 'I'd have thrown her out'; 'I think I might have killed her'; 'I would have taken him apart.' Frequently, this led men to ponder the differences between men and women, and, as several of them put it, men seem to accept loss more easily than women; women don't accept loss, they 'try not to lose.' Others thought that it was because women knew how to fight back with words, because words, not brawn, have always been their only defence. 'Different things are important – men don't give a damn where the hell the screwing gets done, whose bed is irrelevant.' Variations on the theme of the bed cropped up again and again. And yet almost all of them said they could understand why this sort of thing might be important to a woman, even though one of them said that he could only really understand why his wife had made such a thing of the bed, because it was the bed that she had bought and paid for!

Even in the light of their own past experience of a saved marriage, several men said that they would not be able to withstand the assault of the other man. Others, however, felt that, having been saved, they would at least try. But again and again, whether apologetically or defiantly, most men insisted on seeing the world as it is, and *not* as we would like it to be. Whether due to conditioning or not – indeed, whatever the cause – most men have a sort of primal understanding, or half-perceived awareness, that it is harder for a woman to keep a man than it is the other way round. This seems to correspond (doubtlessly in some unscientific way) with that sort of primal understanding, or half-perceived fear most women feel whatever the circumstances, 'he might leave me . . .' No one denies that the sexual arousal mechanism differs between male and female, though recent studies suggest that this philosophy is changing. Men do not look at other men in terms of their potential threat quotient as women do.

It may be that some aspects of human behaviour are not to be explained scientifically, because if they were, something of the necessary mystery or magic that defines, and defies, the differences between the sexes would be lost. Or, as Bud Anderson, a property developer aged 64, said, 'By and large most men are not as curious about human emotion as most women. Men honour contracts, women honour emotions.'

But to switch for a moment to the interpretation of the Woman versus Woman conflict by those husbands who did not defect, the emphasis fell on what the wives did *not* do, rather than what they did. 'She didn't load me with guilt'; 'She didn't blame me for what had happened'; 'She didn't say a word against Ann'; 'She didn't go to pieces'; 'She didn't let me see how she suffered'; 'She never let on to the kids'; 'She never asked how I could do this to her.'

Speaking of relationships with Other Women that could well have ended the marriage, many husbands, needless to say, said they didn't know whether their wives knew or not, their wives had 'looked the other way', or 'kept their eyes shut', or 'pretended not to know', or 'knew what men are like', and so on. They didn't know whether their wives knew or not, and at the time, they didn't care. But they believed their wives *must* have known, though, 'Thank God she never brought it to a head'; 'She didn't insist on a confrontation'; 'Her silence averted catastrophe.'

All the same, the following examples of what wives actually did all seem to point to the way *these wives succeeded in diminishing the ecstasy – or affair – without diminishing the man.*

'She told me that it happened to most men. She named names'; 'She explained that it was not because of our marriage – it was something that happened to men'; and there were many variations on the theme that he should tell the Other Woman that she loved him, too, and would wait for him, even if she couldn't guarantee how long she would wait, while others said they would wait forever.

Perhaps this tactic can best be summarized by what Oliver, an advertising executive aged 34, married for ten years, said of his wife Kim: 'It takes one hell of a woman to do that for a man. To tell him she'd wait forever. To give him such a sense of security.' As Oliver explained, 'It was only fair to Jen to tell her how Kim felt.' (Sincere or otherwise, Kim's tactic worked.)

Like many such husbands who have experienced ecstasy, Oliver speaks of his wife with something closely akin to reverence. True, the affair with Jen happened two years ago, and time dims emotions, but even so, it is clear that these men emerged with a far greater respect for their wives than they had had hitherto. Perhaps their wives paid too high a price for that respect – perhaps not – in any case it should put paid to the belief that for a wife to fight for her own husband she has to lose her self-respect.

Bert, a computer expert aged 55, speaking of his wife, Avril, 50, said that it was his wife's revelation that this had happened to his own father that had, as he put it, 'stopped him in his tracks.' In one master stroke Avril removed both his sense of guilt and his sense of the miraculous. Avril's mother-in-law had confided in Avril at the time – why, Bert even knew the Other Woman! And what his father had seen in her he could not, to this day, imagine! It happened long ago, and the protagonists of that affair have long since died, and at the early stages of this research it would not have occurred to the author to doubt Avril's account of her dead father-in-law's affair. Now the author forbears comment – Bert believed it.

Matthew's wife, Claudie, told him that he would have had

to have been either gay or queer if he was going to resist the kind of advances Annette made. It wasn't his fault; it was all her fault. 'She made me see what Annette's husband was like, too. I took a good look at him, and Claudie was right, he was terrified of her. Talk about a narrow escape!'

Of course these were the wives who managed to keep some sort of communication with their husbands, often even after the husband had defected – a Herculean task indeed. It is clear that to be effective it must aim for pragmatism and avoid sentiment. This is evidenced by all those women who did not ask '*how could he do this to me?*'

We are here concerned with the husbands' accounts of their wives' successful campaigns and therefore with successful communication and, though the lines of communication are usually the first to fall, it would seem that communication can and does take place far more commonly than has been supposed. In other words, however wounded, however frightened, however distraught, or however jealous the wife is, it would seem that the lines of communication continued to function if only because the wife somehow contrived not to humiliate her husband, protecting thereby not only his self-respect but her own. And sometimes, knowing even that defecting from the Other Woman to return home might in itself imply loss of face, more than one husband was told that 'it takes a big man to change his mind.'

For these are the wives who elected not to go to war with their husbands, but with the Other Woman. The methods referred to above are judged in terms of their effectiveness and do not take into account elements of 'right' or 'wrong', or other factors such as the paternalistic society of the West. After all, the Other Woman would have been in a stronger position if she had believed that the wife was willing to surrender. Be that as it may, one must not lose sight of the fact that during the course of the strategy of diplomacy, the prize of the war was also turned into an ambassador in charge of relaying selected vital information to the enemy. In the Woman versus Woman conflict both women use the man in the middle as a courier's ambassador, as witness all those Other Women who suggested that the wife ought to be put out of her misery and told the truth, that is that she was no longer required. And then again, perhaps the wife who asked her husband, 'Don't go sneaking off on me. Tell me what you decide' also calculated that this message would not only be conveyed to the Other Woman, but to his friends, thus procuring for him their envy, as well. 'I am the envy of all me mates!' one man said. And how proud he was of this, as he was of his wife.

Though it is tempting to go into the many theories of men who are successful with women, who speak of themselves as Don Juans or Casanovas, just as they speak of 'my women' and so on, the comment of Ken, a highly attractive bachelor in his early forties in the media business, is revealing enough to merit a brief mention. 'I don't know what made me do this the first time I did it, but when I pretended at a party that I was married, I found that women were more interested in me than they had been. I've done this quite a few times since then, and it's always seemed to make me more interesting!' No doubt because the married man is the perfect temporary ecstasy object.

Benjamin, aged 58, and a highly successful businessman, has had many Other Women in his life, and it was only his most important affair that lasted seven years and two months that made him leave his wife, Ruth, to live with Annabel, twenty-five years younger than he. As he rather laconically put it,

'Fortunately, however, my wife made it possible for me to return with dignity. She knew that Annabel and I had never met as equals – as adults – during those seven years. We could not endure one another, and after two months, I left. It was Annabel's quality of innocence that had so attracted me – for seven years – and though we had been away together, frequently for several days at a time, I never knew how restricting it could become.'

Here Benjamin could not contain his shudder. He went on to say,

'You know, I often give younger men advice on these matters. Older men, too. I tell them that a man can be just as greedy for sex as he can be for money. And then I go on to explain to them what I call the Rule of Nature. The new excites and stimulates performance, but only if you keep it new. I try to warn them that to exchange a mistress for a wife is to end up with a wife and without a mistress. In fact you end up with not one, but with two *wives*. A plurality of mistresses by all means, but never, sir, a plurality of wives. And some of them see sense, some of them do.'

Jack, a pharmacist aged 38, did not even attempt to conceal his sense of self-disgust. 'So you leave the wife to marry the girlfriend – so you bought yourself three years' excitement – and then what? Another wife! Then what . . .?'

Needless to say, those husbands who had left bitter, strifetorn homes did not express regret. But, almost always, those who had left a comfortable marriage in the expectation of an ecstatic marriage expressed not only regret but also bitter self-contempt.

Derek is one of the many men interviewed who realized his previous marriage had not been been unhappy only *after* he had remarried. His case is particularly interesting because he and his first wife, Lynne, had agreed on a vasectomy.

'We had three children and didn't want more,' said Derek, sounding puzzled. 'I never thought of divorce, then. How was I to know I was going to meet Marie? Or that Lynne would force me to choose? We've been married for a year now, and all I can say is that at least there won't be any kids from this marriage. Marie's got three of her own as it is. Jesus, it's a mess! What a mess!'

Would he go back to Lynne? 'She won't even talk to me, so that's out. I never should have left in the first place!'

The complications of new children, previous children, to say nothing of financial obligations that force many a second wife to go to work to support his previous family and ex-wife, seem to impose pressures that are as relentless as they are pitiless. And all too often there is the added burden of a guilt that won't go away even if the children have. Sadly, almost unfailingly, most men who had exchanged peace and comfort and even boredom for that elixir of ecstasy found themselves cheated, disillusioned and confused. It would seem that ecstasy, as priceless as it is ephemeral, is above price, as it is above all else if only because it doesn't last long enough to withstand measurement.

Although this chapter is concerned in the main with the man in the middle it may not be inappropriate to end with the words of Halena Szpiro, a wise, keen and experienced observer of life.

> 'When a husband leaves his wife everyone automatically assumes it's for pure sex. But when a woman leaves her husband it's rare for people to think it's for pure sex. Women don't leave for sex – they're too clever for that – but men do.'

Bibliography

Alvarez, A., *Life after Marriage* (Macmillan London Limited, 1982).

Anderson, Michael (ed.), *Sociology of the Family* (Penguin Books, 1980).

Appleton, William S., *Fathers and Daughters* (Papermac, 1982).

Bach, George R. and Wyden, Peter, *The Intimate Enemy* (Avon Books, 1970).

Bailey, Caroline, *Beginning in the Middle* (Quartet Books, 1982).

Baker, Nancy C., *New Lives for Former Wives* (Anchor Press/Doubleday, New York, 1980).

Barry, Kathleen, *Female Sexual Slavery* (Avon Books, 1979).

Bauer, Bernard A., *Woman and Love*, Vols I and II (Liveright Publishing Corp., 1955).

Benson, Michael, *Marriage at Risk* (Peter Davies, 1958).

Berger, Charles R., 'Sex Differences Related to Self-esteem Factor Structure', *Journal of Consulting and Clinical Psychology*, vol. 32, no. 4, pp. 442–6, 1968.

Bergman, Edgar, *The Compleat Chauvinist* (Macmillan Publishing Co. Inc., New York, 1982).

Bernard, Jessie, *The Future of Marriage* (Yale University Press, 1982).

Berne, Eric, *Sex in Human Loving* (Simon & Schuster, 1970).

Blanch, Lesley, *The Wider Shores of Love* (John Murray, 1954).

Botwin, Carole, *Love Lives* (Bantam Books, 1983).

Boudouris, James, 'Homicide and the Family', *Journal of Marriage and the Family* pp. 667–76, November 1971.

Bowlby, John, *Attachment and Loss:* Vol. I. *Attachment*. Vol. II. *Separation, Anxiety and Anger* (Penguin Books, 1981).

Bowskill, Derek, *Single Parents* (Futura Publications Ltd., 1980).

Brannen, Julia M., 'Seeking Help for Marital Problems: A Conceptual Approach', *British Journal of Social Work*, vol. 10, pp. 457–70, 1980.

Bromley, P. M., *Family Law* (Butterworths, 1966).

Brothers, Joyce, *What Every Woman Should Know About Men* (Simon & Schuster, New York, 1981).

Brown, Helen Gurley, *Having it All* (Simon & Schuster/Linden Press, New York, 1982).

Brownmiller, Susan, *Against Our Will* (Secker & Warburg, 1975).

Chesser, Eustace, *The Cost of Loving* (Methuen, 1964).

Chessler, Phyllis, *About Men* (The Women's Press Ltd., 1978). *Women and Madness* (Avon Books, 1973). *Women, Money and Power* (William Morrow & Co. Inc., New York, 1970).

Chester, Robert, 'The Duration of Marriage to Divorce', *The British Journal of Sociology*, vol. 22, pp. 172–82, 1971.

Cobb, John, 'Morbid Jealousy', *British Journal of Hospital Medicine*, pp. 511–18, May, 1979.

Cobb, J. P. and Marks, J. M., 'Morbid Jealousy Featuring as Obsessive – Compulsive Neurosis: Treatment by Behavioural Psychotherapy', *British Journal of Psychiatry*, vol. 134, pp. 301–5, 1979.

Cooper, David, *The Death of the Family* (Allen Lane, 1971).

Davenport, Diana, *One Parent Families* (Sheldon Press, 1982).

Denholtz, Elaine, *Having It Both Ways* (Stein & Day, 1981).

de Riencourt, Amoury, *Sex and Power in History* (Dell Publishing Co., 1974).

Dickson, Annie, *A Woman in Your Own Right* (Quartet Books, 1982).

Dineen, Jacqueline, *Going Solo* (Unwin Paperbacks, 1982).

Docherty, John P. and Ellis, Jean, 'A New Concept and Finding in Morbid Jealousy', *American Journal Psychiatry*, pp. 133–6, June, 1976.

Dominian, J., *Marital Breakdown* (Penguin Books, 1979). 'Introduction to Marital Pathology', *British Medical Journal*, 18 & 25 August 1979, 1, 8, 15, 22 & 29 September 1979.

Dowling, Colette, *The Cinderella Complex* (Summit Books, 1981).

Drummond, Maggie, *How to Survive as a Second Wife* (Robson Books, 1981).

Drury, Michael, *Advice to a Young Wife from an Old Mistress* (Doubleday, 1968).

Dworkin, Andrea, *Pornography* (The Women's Press Ltd., 1981).

Dyer, Clare and Berlins, Marcel, *Living Together* (Hamlyn Paperbacks, 1982).

Eichenbaum, Luise and Orbach, Susie, *Outside In . . . Inside Out* (Penguin Books, 1982).

Evans, William N., 'The Eye of Jealousy and Envy', *Psychoanalytic Review*, vol. 62, 1975.

Eysenck, J. H. J., *Sex and Personality* (Abacus, 1978).

Farber, Leslie H., *Lying, Despair, Jealousy, Envy, Sex, Suicide, Drugs and One Good Life* (Harper Colophon Books, 1976).

Fischer, Helen E., *The Sex Contract* (Granada Publishing, 1982).

Flach, Frederic F., *The Secret Strengths of Depression* (Lippincott, 1974).

Foster, George M., 'The Anatomy of Envy: A Study in Symbolic Behaviour', *Current Anthropology*, vol. 13, no. 2, pp. 165–201, April, 1972.

Friday, Nancy, *Men in Love* (Arrow Books Ltd., 1981). *My Mother/My Self* (Fontana, 1979).

Friedan, Betty, *The Feminine Mystique* (Dell Publishing Co. Inc., 1963). *The Second Stage* (Summit Books, 1981).

Gathorne-Hardy, Jonathan, *Love, Sex, Marriage, Divorce* (Jonathan Cape Ltd., 1981).

Gilder, George, 'In Defence of Monogamy', *Commentary*, vol. 58, no. 5, November 1974.

Guttentag, Marcia and Secord, Paul F., *Too Many Women?* (Sage, 1983).

Haddon, Celia, *The Limits of Sex* (Michael Joseph, 1982).

Hallberg, Edmond C., *The Gray Itch* (Warner Books, 1980).

Heath, Stephen, *The Sexual Fix* (The Macmillan Press Ltd., 1982).

Hite, Shere, *The Hite Report* (Dell Publishing Co. Inc., 1981). *The Hite Report on Male Sexuality* (Macdonald, Futura Publishers, 1981).

Hornstein, Harvey A., *Cruelty and Kindness* (A Spectrum Book, 1976).

Hurvitz, Nathan, 'The Sociologist as a Marital and Family Therapist', *American Behavioral Scientist*, vol. 23, no. 3, pp. 557–76, March/April 1979.

Ingham, Mary, *Now We Are Thirty* (Eyre Methuen Ltd., 1981).

'J', *The Sensuous Woman* (W. H. Allen, 1971).

James, Wendy and Kedgley, Susan Jane, *The Mistress* (Abelard-Schuman, 1973).

Jenner, Heather, *Marriages Are Made On Earth* (David & Charles Ltd., 1979).
Johnson, Ralph E., 'Some Correlates of Extramarital Coitus', *Journal of Marriage and the Family*, pp. 449–56, August, 1970.
Jones, Ann, *Women Who Kill* (Fawcett/Columbine Books, 1981).
Jongeward, Dorothy and Scott, Drue, *Women as Winners* (Addison-Wesley Publishing Co. Inc., 1976).
Kitzinger, Sheila, *Women as Mothers* (Fontana, 1978).
Krantzler, Mel, *Creative Divorce* (Signet Books, 1975). *Creative Marriage* (McGraw-Hill, 1981).
Kreitler, Peter and Bruns, Bill, *Affair Prevention* (Macmillan Publishing Co. Inc., New York, 1981).
Krupinoki, Jerzy, Marshall, Elizabeth and Yule, Valerie, 'Patterns of Marital Problems in Marriage Guidance Clients', *Journal of Marriage and The Family*, pp. 138–42, February, 1970.
Lake, Tony, *Affairs* (Open Books, 1979).
Lasch, Christopher, *The Culture of Narcissism* (W. W. Norton Inc., New York, 1978).
Laski, Marghanita, *Everyday Ecstasy* (Thames & Hudson, 1980).
Lazarus, Arnold, *In the Mind's Eye* (Rawson Associates, Publishers, 1977).
Legman, G., *Rationale of the Dirty Joke* (Jonathan Cape, 1969).
Levinson, Daniel J., *The Seasons of a Man's Life* (Alfred A. Knopf, 1978).
Lewis, C. S., *The Four Loves* (Fontana Books, 1981).
Lilar, Suzanne, *Aspects of Love* (Thames & Hudson, London, 1965).
Llewellyn-Jones, Derek, *Every Man* (Oxford University Press, 1982).
McGill, Michael E., *The 40 to 60 Year Old Male* (Simon & Schuster, New York, 1980).
McGinley, Phyllis, *The Province of the Heart* (Viking, 1959).
Maddox, Brenda, *Married and Gay* (Harcourt Brace Jovanovich, Publishers, New York, 1982). *Step-Parenting* (Unwin Paperbacks, 1980).
May, Rollo, *Love and Will* (Fontana Library, 1972).
Mitchell, Ann K., *Someone to Turn to* (Aberdeen University Press, 1981).
Morgan, Elaine, *The Descent of Women* (Stein & Day Publishers, New York, 1980).
Mostyn, F. E., *Marriage and the Law* (Oyez Publishing Ltd., 1976).

Mount, Ferdinand, *The Subversive Family* (Jonathan Cape, London, 1982).
Neely, James C., *Gender* (Simon & Schuster, New York, 1981).
Nicholson, John, *A Question of Sex* (Fontana Paperbacks, 1979).
Nicolson, Nigel, *Portrait of a Marriage* (Weidenfeld & Nicolson, 1973).
O'Neill, Nena, *The Marriage Premise* (Evans, 1977).
Phillips, Estelle M., 'Psychology and Marriage Counselling', *Bulletin British Psychology Society*, vol. 33, pp. 340–41, 1977.
Pietropinto, A. and Simenauer, J., *Husbands and Wives* (Berkley Books, New York, 1981).
Pinta, Emil R., 'Pathological Tolerance', *American Journal of Psychiatry*, pp. 135–6, June, 1978.
Reiss, Ivan L., Anderson, Ronald E., Sponaugle, G. C., 'Multivariate Model of the Determinants of Extramarital Sexual Permissiveness', *Journal of Marriage and the Family*, pp. 395–411, May, 1980.
Renvoize, Jean, *Web of Violence* (Routledge & Kegan Paul, 1978).
Rico-Velasco, J. and Mynko, L., 'Suicide and Marital Status: A Changing Relationship', *Journal of Marriage and The Family*, pp. 239–44, May, 1973.
Rowbotham, Sheila, *Women's Consciousness in a Man's World* (Pelican Books, 1973).
Russell, Bertrand, *Marriage and Morals* (Unwin Books, 1970).
Russianoff, Penelope, *Why Do I Think I Am Nothing Without a Man?* (Bantam Books, 1982).
Ryan, Kevin, *Making a Marriage* (St Martin's Press, 1982).
Sands, Melissa, *The Mistress Survival Manual* (Berkley Books, 1981). *The Second Wife Survival Manual* (Berkley Books, 1982).
Scarf, Maggie, *Unfinished Business* (Doubleday & Co. Inc., 1980).
Schalin, Lars J., 'On the Problem of Envy', *Scandinavian Psychoanalytical Review*, vol. 2, pp. 133–58, 1979.
Schapera, Isaacs, *Married Life in an African Tribe* (Pelican Books, 1971).
Schnall, Maxine, *Limits* (Clarkson N. Potter Inc., 1981).
Seeman, Mary V., 'Pathological Jealousy', *Psychiatry*, vol. 42, pp. 351–61, November, 1979.
Sexton, Linda Gray, *Between Two Worlds* (William Morrow, 1979).
Shain, Merle, *Some Men are More Perfect than Others* (Lippincott, 1973).
Sheehy, Gail, *Pathfinders* (Sidgwick & Jackson Ltd., 1982). *Passages* (E. P. Dutton, 1976).

Shettel-Neuber, J., Bryson, Jeff B. and Young, Leanne E., 'Physical Attractiveness of the "Other Person" and Jealousy', *Personality and Social Psychology Bulletin*, vol. 4, no. 4, 1978.
Shorter, Edward, *The Making of the Modern Family* (Fontana Books, 1979).
Skynner, A. C. Robin, *One Flesh: Separate Persons* (Constable & Co. Ltd., 1979).
Stone, Lawrence, *The Family, Sex and Marriage in England 1500–1800* (Pelican Books, 1979).
Talese, Gay, *Thy Neighbour's Wife* (Pan Books, 1981).
Tanner, Tony, *Adultery in the Novel* (The Johns Hopkins University Press, 1979).
Thornes, Barbara and Collard, Jean, *Who Divorces?* (Routledge & Kegan Paul, 1979).
Tiesman, Mark W. and Mosher, Donald L., 'Jealous Conflict in Dating Couples', *Psychological Reports*, vol. 42, pp. 1211–16, April, 1978.
Trieve, Lynette, *Learning to Leave* (Contemporary Books, 1982).
Tweedie, Jill, *In the Name of Love* (Jonathan Cape, 1979).
Vail, Lauren O., *Divorce* (Sovereign Books, 1979).
Villar, Esther, *The Polygamous Sex* (W. H. Allen, 1976).
Wagner, Jon, 'Jealousy, Extended Intimacies and Sexual Affirmation etc.', *A Review of General Semantics*, pp. 269–88, September, 1976.
Wanderer, Z. and Cabot, T., *Letting Go* (Warner Books, 1979).
Weisberg, Miriam I., 'Early Treatment of Infidelity in the Neuromatic Man', *Social Casework* (Family Service Association of America) vol. 51, pp. 358–67, June, 1970.
Wheeler-Bennet, Joan, *Women at the Top* (Peter Owen, London, 1977).
White, Gregory L., 'Jealousy and Partner's Perceived Motives for Attraction to a Rival', *Social Psychology Quarterly*, vol. 44, no. 1, pp. 24–30, 1981.
Whitehurst, Robert N., 'Violence Potential in Extramarital Sexual Responses', *Journal of Marriage and the Family*, pp. 683–91.
Wilson, Glenn, *Love and Instinct* (Temple Smith, London, 1981).
Wilson, Glenn and Nias, David, *Love's Mysteries: The Psychology of Sexual Attraction* (Open Books, 1976).
Wolfe, Linda, *The Cosmo Report* (Corgi, 1982).

Index

Note: OW in index refers to Other Woman